DANNIELLE BLUMENTHAL

On Government

Copyright © 2023 by Dannielle Blumenthal

All rights reserved. No part of this publication may be reproduced, stored or transmitted in any form or by any means, electronic, mechanical, photocopying, recording, scanning, or otherwise without written permission from the publisher. It is illegal to copy this book, post it to a website, or distribute it by any other means without permission.

Dannielle Blumenthal asserts the moral right to be identified as the author of this work.

Dannielle Blumenthal has no responsibility for the persistence or accuracy of URLs for external or third-party Internet Websites referred to in this publication and does not guarantee that any content on such Websites is, or will remain, accurate or appropriate.

Designations used by companies to distinguish their products are often claimed as trademarks. All brand names and product names used in this book and on its cover are trade names, service marks, trademarks and registered trademarks of their respective owners. The publishers and the book are not associated with any product or vendor mentioned in this book. None of the companies referenced within the book have endorsed the book.

Although the author has made every effort to ensure that the information in this book was correct at press time and while this publication is designed to provide accurate information in regard to the subject matter covered, the author assumes no responsibility for errors, inaccuracies, omissions, or any other inconsistencies herein and hereby disclaim any liability to any party for any loss, damage, or disruption caused by errors or omissions, whether such errors or omissions result from negligence, accident, or any other cause.

Further, new information frequently causes old information to be rendered obsolete. The reader should exercise caution in reading this "snapshot in time," keeping in mind that it represents the available information and observations available during a limited time window and from a very limited knowledge base.

The author does not make any guarantee or other promise as to any results that may be obtained from using the content of this book. This publication is meant as a source of information for the reader, but it is not meant as a substitute for direct expert assistance and independent verification. If such level of assistance is required, the services of a competent professional should be sought. To the maximum extent permitted by law, the author disclaims any and all liability in the event any information, commentary, analysis, opinions, advice and/or recommendations contained in this book prove to be inaccurate, incomplete or unreliable, or result in any investment or other losses.

Readers should not judge the importance of a topic based on the author's interest in it, nor assume that a topic is important merely because it is included in this book.

All subjects mentioned in the book are presumed innocent until proven guilty in a court of law or administrative action and any and all crimes are alleged until a court or regulatory agency finds otherwise.

The purpose of this book is to benefit the public through criticism, comment, news reporting, teaching, scholarship, education and research. Under Section 107 of the Copyright Act of 1976, this work therefore falls under the doctrine of "fair use," which provides for the legal, non-licensed citation or incorporation of copyrighted material in another author's work. "Fair use" relies on a a four-factor balancing test that includes the purpose and character of use; the nature of the copyrighted work; the amount and substantiality of the portion taken; and the effect of the use upon the potential market. Any copyrighted material appearing in this book is believed by the author to fall under the doctrine of "fair use."

The views and opinions expressed by the author are those of the author alone. They do not, and are not intended to, officially or unofficially represent any ideology, agenda, individual, organization, federal agency, or the government as a whole.

The author has not been paid or otherwise compensated in exchange for expressing a particular point of view. Nothing in this work should be construed to imply that the author authorizes, supports, endorses or sponsors any product or service.

The material covered in this work encompasses matters related to gender, race, religion, class, and so on. The author is aware that unconscious bias is a real phenomenon and has attempted to review and correct for any assertions that may be based in personal attributes and identity rather than objective fact. The author has no malign intent and asks in advance for the reader's forgiveness for any missteps or errors in this area.

Finally, this book deals with sensitive themes in a direct manner. This may be triggering for trauma survivors or people who have been through difficult experiences, their loved ones, empathic individuals, and others. The author urges the reader to consult with a competent mental health professional if they experience difficult emotions around the subject matter.

First edition

This book was professionally typeset on Reedsy.
Find out more at reedsy.com

Dedicated to my family.

Contents

Preface

I have been a government worker for most of my professional career, though it isn't what I intended to do with my life. At first reluctantly, then doggedly, and now passionately, I bring everything I have to the table. These articles reflect my journey primarily during the years 2007-2018. (As such, many are dated; please make note of this as you read.)

Some of the lessons in this book are from published research. Most of them come from life experience and observing the good and bad actions of others. I am grateful to everyone who has taught me how to be a good civil servant.

My prayer for you is that you take these articles, read them or skim them, and use them to inform your own work for the government, in any capacity.

If you don't work for the government but simply have an interest in the subject, I hope that you will see how complicated it is to actually work here, and avoid stereotyping civil servants in the way the media tends to portray us.

My feeling has always been that, as Anne Frank said, "people are really good at heart." And in the government, most people want very much to serve the public. This, more than anything else, is what distinguishes civil servants as a group.

Acknowledgement

With gratitude to God.

I

Branding

1

Brand New: Ten Reasons Every Agency Should Focus On What Makes It Special

Agencies with strong brands enjoy at least 10 advantages over their weakly branded counterparts.

Top talent: People want to work for agencies with strong brands, and their employees are proud to be there. As reported in the book *Brand Warfare: 10 Rules for Building the Killer Brand* by David F. D'Alessandro and Michele Owens (McGraw–Hill, 2001), Fortune magazine found in 2000 that the average number of job applicants per opening was twice as high for companies on its Top 10 Most Admired list as for those on its 100 Best Companies to Work For list.

Improved reputation: Strongly branded agencies have improved credibility among key stakeholders. The perception is that they're doing a good job at achieving their mission.

Leadership: A strong brand implies that the chief executive officer knows how to guide and direct the agency based on its mission, core values and culture, and managers know how to direct front-line employees.

Citizen compliance: People are more likely to comply with rules set forth by a name they know, recognize and understand than one they are unfamiliar with.

Customer service: The strong brand instills in employees core values that lead them to listen better and respond to citizens.

Citizen education: Employees have a clearer sense of mission and communicate it consistently in guidelines and educational documents they issue to the public.

Decision-making: The vision, mission, values and common culture clarify for employees at all levels how to make decisions about matters large and small.

Reduced confusion: Customers are better able to distinguish a well-branded agency from others that are a former iteration or sound similar.

Internal communication: Employees are united by a common vision, values and culture. They communicate openly about matters of importance.

Funding: Congress is more apt to fund the programs of a strong brand, based on a perception that the agency deserves significant appropriations.

How do you build a strong brand like those enjoyed by the FBI, Secret Service and Coast Guard? It starts with brand assessment, that is, finding out how your key stakeholders see you versus how you see yourself. For example, you may think your agency is "citizen-centric," but the public might see it as remote and indifferent.

Next comes brand strategy. Based on research inside and outside the agency, you articulate the vision, core values, common culture, positioning and other key attributes. You focus more on the vision, values and culture because you already have a name and a mission.

Third are brand communication guidelines: How do you want your graphics, Web site, press materials, recruitment documents and other materials to look? The goal is to arrive at a consistent identity that allows for some variation to keep things interesting. You want to reinforce the vision, mission, values and culture in all you say and do.

Fourth is a brand launch. No matter how well you do your research, think through your strategy and sharpen your presentation, you'll need a change implementation program to prepare your employees and customers for a shift in the way you communicate about yourself.

Everyone, at every level, should be encouraged and rewarded for living the brand in a way that will be visible both on the inside and on the outside. Some organizations even produce a brand reference book to guide employees in this endeavor.

Finally, you'll need a brand management system-ongoing measurement and tracking of how the brand is doing. This can range from how well identity and image standards are upheld to measurements of the brand's reputation as portrayed in the media to programs that assess how well employees are upholding the values established by the brand. The key is to tie a business outcome metric to a combination of elements of the brand.

If you haven't thought about your brand lately, or have discarded the work you've done on it recently, now might be the time to pick it back up and do some new thinking. Your brand can provide an opportunity to meet and even exceed your agency's strategic goals.

From Branding to Social Media

Branding has evolved from an advertising-driven discipline to one that is led by social media. This is a scenario in which the user dictates the nature of the brand rather than the brand dictating an image to the user.

The idea that people would be "talking back" to, co-creating, and even overriding Big Brands was unheard of in the age of "Mad Men," but we are seeing this scenario come to pass.

The trend began with a move from solely externally focused branding to externally and internally focused communication in which the brand was said to have "values" that translated to all stakeholders. It is continuing as message senders recognize they must have more than the public's attention in order to be successful.

It's about having a pool of information or content that the user reaches into, pulls something out of, negotiates with in their mind, and returns in the form of an opinion, a creative piece of content, a mashup – a.k.a. "curation."

In the future public engagement is going to mean a fundamental change in the nature of public engagement activities. This post describes what those are, in the form of a Q&A I posted to Quora.

The bottom line is, if public engagement is your goal, then you are in effect selling a message.

To sell that message effectively, you must be completely focused on the user – what they want to hear, how they want to hear it, and what methods make the transmission of information credible.

As the public grows more and more comfortable talking to each other and talking back, the traditional "shove a message down their throat with a press release" is going to be worse than irrelevant. While government will always need to be concerned with providing validated information, its job is not to decide what information the public "should" want to hear but rather to give them the information they demand.

Consequently, the job of the outreach specialist is to find interested parties where they congregate, offer consumable information there, and participate in the conversation that ensues.

The definition of success, in this environment, is a robust conversation – one in which disagreement is not only tolerated but celebrated – one in which all are invited to participate.

Here is the Q&A.

Question

Who originally came up with things like 'brand values', 'missions', 'visions' and models like the 'brand pyramid'? I'm interested in the history of brand strategy. I've read lots of books on brand strategy, and none of them talk about where these ways of doing things came from. Did they come from *someone*? From P&G? Or elsewhere? – From the Brand Strategy topic page, Quora

Answer

(originally posted by me to Quora.com)

Summary

Concepts tying the brand to a personality, or a set of values or a kind of mission, did not go mainstream until the late 2000s and probably coincide with the popularization of Facebook.

It was only then that – due to social media – the wall between the personal and the professional crumbled to the point that one had to espouse certain personal values in order for those to be taken seriously as part of one's external image.

As far as models, they became popular around the mid-2000s as the term "branding" gained currency and everyone wanted to claim a piece of the pie with their own 'methodology'. This especially true around brand equity models.

Detail

This is my perspective as someone who has worked in branding since 2000. I was hired as VP & Editorial Director for the Brand Futures Group that year; it's a small trendspotting think-tank that was part of Young & Rubicam. (Later they were renamed The Intelligence Factory).

The focus back then was strictly on branding as an offshoot

of advertising. That was it: Ads came first, ads built brands, brands added value, and we predicted the trends that would make ads meaningful.

When we did research on branding we focused on consumer behavior – not on the relationship between the organization and the employee. It would have been unheard of to call that "branding."

In 2001 I was hired by a small company in Washington, DC called The Brand Consultancy which focused on something called "internal branding." This is where you get the whole language of vision, mission, brand values, and so on.

This was completely fascinating to me as a native sociologist and latent organizational development specialist. In the year that I spent working for Y&R I thought that branding was about predicting social behavior. I wrote things like "one day we'll show allegiance to our favorite brands with tattoos" and "we'll be seeing the emergence of single-on-purpose women as a target audience".

But TBC did something completely different. They talked about the brand on the inside, with "Brand Bibles" and training books and concepts like "operationalizing the brand."

The company actually represented a merger between two smaller consultancies, and I had the opportunity to learn directly from the principals regarding how they coached, poked and prodded CEOs into branding not the products but the workforce.

As I recall the business was divided between advertising-type services (e.g. logo); brand-type services (e.g. assessment; strategy); and hybrids (e.g. a well designed Brand Bible).

Key Concepts

It was also around this time that I learned about concepts like brand transparency and corporate social responsibility. It became clear to me that every company would have to embrace these as part of their strategic communication plans.

I also led an early social network on Yahoo! Groups where we discussed these topics internationally; wrote articles for a website called Page on AllAboutBranding; and continued researching and writing even after taking a job with the Federal government.

Brand Values Over The Years

- The Federal position I received in 2003 was with the Office of the Comptroller of the Currency as a writer-editor in Internal Communications. While there, I obtained a graduate certificate in Organization Development and set about creating "advertorials" aimed at internal audiences to "brand" the agency to them. I also became involved in best practices groups that espoused early forms of what was soon to go mainstream – "employee first" brand thinking. I even produced an Amazon.com internal rating system for newsletter articles to promote transparency and engagement, but it was rapidly shot down a few years ahead of its time.
- Around 2005 I was hired to work in the Department of Homeland Security's Customs and Border Protection, but neither there nor in my first federal job were the words "internal branding" ever uttered. They literally thought of the brand as the name and logo – nothing else. I even

did a mission integration project – but it was never called "internal branding."

- Around 2009 "employer branding" became important as a tool for recruitment and to that end "internal branding" involved a discussion of mission, vision and values.
- Also around this time social media began to go really mainstream, although initial use was as a means to "spam" the community with one-way messaging.
- By 2012 things had definitively shifted. I worked for USAID, and it became incredibly important to senior leadership that employees believe in the brand just as much as external parties did. While there, I personally helped lead a mission and values initiative aimed at rediscovering who we were – and in the process raising productivity and morale.
- Similarly, in my position at The National Archives, that concept of embodying a set of values was critical. We have an entire internal social network where discussions frequently take place about living up to our mission and core values.

Looking Ahead

In the future I think things are going to go even further, as people demand to look behind the curtain at the brand and mistrust the "official word" in all its forms.

It's really about fostering a conversation between social media and branding, understanding that you cannot be fully authentic all the time nor would you want to be projecting an artificial image.

Three basic changes will go mainstream:

1. People will want to hear from ordinary members of the organization – NOT "flacks," e.g. public relations representatives. This "brand authenticity" will be demanded. Those who do not comply will be mercilessly made fun of, discredited or ignored. Eventually, for the most part, ordinary staff will be encouraged to speak freely about the company rather than having the company speak for them.
2. Disagreements by staff that are expressed in public will not be cause for alarm. It will be acknowledged that having your own ideas is a sign of credibility and will actually make the organization more engaging.
3. Social media strategy will assume prime importance to brand strategy. It will consist of finding where the conversation is taking place, responding to the questions that users have, and accepting their criticism respectfully. This is the complete opposite of "projecting" a false brand image which has been the traditional cornerstone of branding and is rapidly falling away.

Landmark Publications Around Y2K

- The Cluetrain Manifesto – which told me it would not be long before people started to talk back to the image makers.
- "Are The Strategic Stars Aligned For Your Brand?" in Harvard Business Review, by Majken and Schultz – I learned that branding is a holistic exercise connecting internal and external audiences.
- "The Brand Called You" in Fast Company, by Tom Peters – I learned that you personally would become the product –

just as much as the product you sell – and how to optimize my "personal brand" accordingly.

- An article I got to later on was Gallup's "The Fifth P" or how people are the un-discussed essential factor in marketing.

3

Government Isn't Just Another Brand To Be Marketed

Recently an interesting debate arose over the fundamental meaning of branding.

The context was a call for volunteers to help with the user interface of the Good Country, a project aimed at making the world more habitable for all.

Conceptually, here's how it works: participants get to "vote" on the elections taking place in other countries. Given the opportunity to weigh in on another nation's governance, they presumably would take the time to actually learn about those countries, form educated opinions, and become more aware of how one nation's actions affect the others. (See the TED Talk.)

The project's founder, Simon Anholt, is known for the concept of "nation branding," also known as "place branding," which seeks to enhance the images of nations or places much the way companies try to bolster the reputations of their products. Nonetheless, Anholt does not view the Good Country as a branding effort.

A policy advisor, Anholt divorced his project from the concept of branding because he sees the latter as an activity related to image, whereas policy has to do with substance:

> "My belief, backed up by much research (nearly 400 billion data points from 10 years of the Nation Brands Index), has long been that there's no such thing as place "branding" and that countries are judged by what they do rather than by what they say about themselves."

In Anholt's view, campaigns limited to superficial symbols are tempting, but ultimately cannot build or rehabilitate a nation's image.

> The temptation for governments to spend taxpayers' and donors' money on logos, slogans and PR campaigns in an attempt to manipulate the images of their countries, cities and regions is a very strong one: but it simply doesn't work and I've never found a single case study to suggest that it does.

Conceptually, Anholt draws the distinction between image-building and more specific goals of boosting tourism or investment, which can be supported through a marketing campaign.

From Anholt's point of view, conflating branding with policy is dangerous because doing so positions the effort as a competitive one, rather than one where we all work together on substantive improvement for mutual gain.

"I'd like to emphasize that the principle of the Good Country is countries trying to be good, not trying to look good, which is why I find the "branding" label to be a dangerous one. Countries need to become gooder (by which I basically mean that governance needs to be understood as a fundamentally collaborative rather than fundamentally competitive discipline) not primarily because it will benefit their images or trade or international relations, but primarily because it's necessary for the future of humanity."

Anholt's research shows that when nations improve their actions, a better image results. He believes this correlation, which he has mentioned publicly, has created some confusion. The bottom line, says Anholt, is that when a country improves its practices, a better brand image results (but it doesn't work the other way around—image efforts alone don't produce a better brand).

For my part, reading this, I was surprised and concerned at the level of dysfunction and waste that would permit branding efforts to be limited to image-building even in 2017. Back in 2001, The Brand Consultancy in Washington was promoting integrated brand building, marrying operation and image. And frankly the U.S. seemed behind the times; see, for example, the 2001 Harvard Business Review article by Mary Jo Hatch and Majken Schultz *Are The Strategic Stars Aligned For Your Corporate Brand?*

In business, it is clear that 360 degree branding improves the bottom line. But in the world of policy and governance, there are many complicating factors at play.

When the world's policymakers come to see that actions speak louder than words, and that positive actions do yield positive results on every level, we will see the end of branding efforts limited to image.

4

On The Distinction Between Messaging & Branding

I just thought I would spend a couple of minutes clearing this one up as the terms tend to be used interchangeably. They're related but somewhat different.

- Messaging = saying something in a very specific way. As in: "We are working with local authorities to ensure citizen safety."
- Branding = creating an impression in people's minds. As in: When you walk into the fitness center, it's glass and mirrors and every employee looks skinny and 22.

Messaging and branding both need to be consistent:

- When different people explain an event the same way, they reinforce one another and increase credibility. (Unless of course they are lying.)
- When all parts of the company, the individual, the product or the service leave you with the same impression,

branding can be said to be taking place in an integrated manner. (Doesn't mean it's a good strategy or that it's working.)

The distinction though is how messaging and branding are carried out.

- Messaging = top down, and from the middle to the center. It's the military paradigm: chain of command.
- Branding = technically formal and structured, but has to appear spontaneous. It can be top-down but works better bottom-up or outside-in. It's organic and people learn the rules then implement them on their own. You cannot force it.

Every communication shop should know and do both messaging and branding. To do it well it's important to be aware of the distinction.

5

How Branding Can Transform Government Customer Service

On Sept. 2, *NextGov* ran a story about the 2016 edition of Forrester Research's Customer Experience Index. The report will cost you $499 to purchase but the article highlights what for me is the main point:

> *The federal government finished dead last among 21 major industries, and had five of the eight worst scores of the 319 brands, leading Forrester to note that government has a "near monopoly on the worst experiences."*

Before commenting on this study, it should be noted that we don't have a clear sense of what the methodology was. Superficially, we know that there were 122,500 adult respondents polled within the past year, asked for input on 319 brands covering 21 major industries. But when you drill down a little deeper, it's important to ask: What exactly were the questions? How were they asked? Was there an opportunity for respondents to expand on their answer? Why this odd number of brands? What constitutes a "major industry?"

Not just that: What is the definition of "customer service" when you're talking about the federal government versus a private, for-profit company? They're not at all the same things, although the features may be similar in some ways. The principal difference, of course, is that the government is charged with both enforcing the law and serving the public, and so customer service in a government context means helping people to navigate a complicated system. The customer is bound to the government; it isn't a voluntary relationship. That person also may be responsible for paying money to the government or otherwise giving something up; it's not a situation where the consumer enters into a voluntary agreement to exchange funds for services.

One more caveat. There are many perspectives you can bring to any situation when you're looking at ways to improve it. A CIO, for example, will argue for better technology. A human resources professional will argue for better staffing and training. We can go down the list and name a range of professional support services that can offer best-practice expertise (public or private-sector) to improve customer service: All of them can be right.

But complexity messes up headlines. Obviously government and private industry are not directly comparable; obviously there are lots of ways to make things better. I want to offer just a few ideas about what branding can do, because I think this discipline is for some strange reason both deeply misunderstood and utterly neglected in the government, no matter how much money has been thrown at it.

First, a definition: Branding is the professional practice of managing others' perceptions of you. It is not reducible to the specific things one does to try and create those perceptions—a name, a brand, a tagline.

Second, a key point of confusion—a paradox: You produce a thing and call it your "brand." That's valid. But the customer also has a perception and that perception is your "brand," too.

Third, the point of branding: You want to align whatever it is that you've created, to the customers' perception of you.

In my mind branding is not really rocket science. It simply requires you to think objectively about how to improve your customers' perceptions of you. It shouldn't cost a lot of money, either: any agency "tiger team" can reorient itself for improvement by asking these types of questions:

How does customer service fit into our identity? Are we a Walmart type agency that everybody recognizes, and so we would do well by copying private-sector mass-market customer service practices? Are we mostly government-to-government and deal with other agencies? Business people? Lawyers? How will we communicate our identity in every interaction such that they understand who we are and what we can do for them in that capacity?

Who are our customer segments? There will inevitably be at least the following: Internal leaders, employees at large, Congress, the media, and the public. But if we drill down further, who do we really need to satisfy? What is the spoken (legal) or unspoken (implicit) "brand promise" we make by virtue of existence?

What does "delivery" of the customer service promise mean? Is it that we've answered a question? Clarified a rule? Does the customer know what they can expect from us?

What is our customers' preferred method of communicating with us? Do they want a formal letter, a quick email, or might they even be happy to interact via Twitter and Facebook? Do they expect us to be active on social media?

What entity does the customer perceive us to be a part of? Do we need to emphasize our own unique identity, or should we fold into something larger and simpler for them to recognize?

Of course this is not an exhaustive list.

The point is that branding forces you to think from an "outside-in" perspective, rather than solely "inside-out." This is helpful as government agencies tend to suffer from an extreme form of myopia, with not only the agency but also its individual parts and subparts thinking of things very much from a narrow perspective.

Branding, with its emphasis on cognizance of the perceptions of others, is a powerful way to reverse that dynamic.

6

Risk Reduction and Branding Are Really About One Thing: Doing the Right Thing

Branding and reputation are integrally related. The one is built on the other. And when your organization operates in an "at risk" way for an extended period of time, you can be sure that both will falter.

How can you prevent such a crisis from occurring? Thinking from a branding point of view, you want to make sure that your organization has someone in charge of constantly keeping watch over its reputation.

UPS teaches us this principle neatly in its new television commercial. It states:

"Everything your customer sees tells a story."

As a private individual, you've lived this a thousand times. When you argue, you close the door and make sure nobody else is around. Your story is told not by you, but by the people who witness you, in your orbit.

We all know this and yet somehow, incomprehensibly,

it appears that many organizations do not operate by this principle. Their actions speak louder than their words, and as a result the customer experience is miserable. For example:

- They Tweet at the customer about the latest improvements, happenings and updates, but don't offer clear, well-researched answers to the customer's most frequently asked questions.
- They do not offer a consistent promise or experience. The website is difficult to navigate. The product quality is uneven.
- They talk about how important people are, how people are "everything" to them, but they overwork and underpay employees, sell inferior products or services, and offer customers little recourse.
- They have a CEO, a CFO, a COO, a CIO and maybe a CMO, but there is no Chief Brand Officer in charge of the overall image and customer experience.

If I were to walk into your organization today, would it seem like a country at war with itself, or like a finely tuned, well-calibrated orchestra?

Don't ask your executives that question. Ask the people who work for and with you. Ask the people who interact with you. Ask your customers. (Or just observe them and record what you see.) There is no neat line between the different types of stakeholders you serve. Rather, your stakeholders tend to cross from one category into another. Today's customer is tomorrow's employee. That employee may leave the company and become a partner of some kind in the future.

Or maybe they will be a competitor. What weaknesses might they use against you?

People talk. You therefore want to make sure that you control the image of your organization—preferably by doing the right thing—at all times.

But since we live in the real world, and people don't always do the right thing it is important to remedy risky situations as soon as they crop up.

This is why every organization should have an Office of Enterprise Risk.

"Risk" from a branding standpoint is anything about the functioning of your business that, left unchecked, has the potential to harm your reputation.

As you do this, it's important to avoid a common misconception. Because often people think that having a good image literally means telling a positive story, hiring employees who will accept unquestioningly everything you say. Nothing could be further than the truth.

Having a good image means understanding that it is impossible to have a good image unless you are constantly on guard for, and correcting, the problems that arise in the normal course of business.

To establish an Office of Enterprise Risk:

- Designate someone to serve as your Chief of Reputation Risk. This is not the Chief Brand Officer, but rather an individual who heads up an Office of Enterprise Risk. Enterprise risk includes cybersecurity, product quality, accounting best practices, hazard management, and so on.

- Explicitly empower employees to tell you when something is wrong.
- Offer a way employees, customers or other stakeholders to report problems anonymously.
- Establish a reputation council, comprised of the risk officers heading up each unique type of organizational risk. It should convene regularly and investigate and respond to reports that come in. At times it might be necessary to hire an outside entity to conduct the investigation.
- Report out regularly, and publicly, on the activities of the reputation watch-guard and council, including a quantitative report at the end of the year that describes the number and types of incidents reported and actions taken.

The notion that someone is always watching may be frightening, but it is an unavoidable fact. Ignoring this poses a risk to the organization's reputation. And without a strong reputation, obviously, marketing and branding efforts will inevitably fall flat.

Think about it from a strategic point of view. Proactively managing your reputation is a smart investment. Rather than waiting for a crisis to blow up in your face—an expensive, chaotic proposition that will inevitably take you away from your core business—invest in preventive maintenance in advance.

Having an Office of Enterprise Risk supports your reputation, and your brand, by engaging trained professionals to monitor and mitigate the most common presenting risks. When they work together, in concert with your Chief Branding Officer, you can communicate in a credible and consistent way about unavoidable issues.

Think about risk—in advance—then mitigate it. Don't live in fear of surprises. That will make your organization one that people trust.

7

Branding Cannot Be Fully Scripted

The business genius Peter Drucker was 100 percent on target when he said that "a business exists to create a customer." But as most of us already know, but maybe don't think about so much (because new ads are sexier than loyalty campaigns) — it's a hell of a lot cheaper, smarter and more efficient to invest in the customers you have than to constantly ignore them in favor of strangers.

And of course, the way you keep your customers delighted, and coming back for more is through consistent, personalized, structured (and yes, sometimes boring and irritating) customer service. Particularly for those who buy the most things for the highest price tag.

Think about it:

- The entirety of your business is your brand. **Not the widgets you think you sell.**
- The entirety of your brand is lodged, living and breathing, in the relationships you have with each and every customer. Dispersed among them. **Not in your brochures,**

or your "brandcuff."

- The relationships you have with each and every customer are unique, they develop over time, and they are real. **Relationships cannot be programmed or scripted.**

I am confident that we are looking at a robotized future, where most of the work is done by automated creatures we have dreamed up in a lab. But the thinking work cannot be delegated.

Do you know what makes terrorist propaganda over social media channels so successful, while efforts to counter them have miserably failed? It is that counter-terrorists refuse to un-handcuff their communicators. For in a system run by terrorists, the only qualification is fanatical loyalty to a simple shared cause that all understand. There is no other litmus test for a Tweet.

New recruits buy into the messages broadcast over social media. Soon, they establish relationships with actual people. They join a shadowy world where they can shed their previous bland identities and immerse themselves in purpose.

How do you fight that? That's the ultimate one-on-one brand-building campaign, and the person standing on the other side of that wall is braying insults with both hands tied behind their back.

The simple fact about branding is that the relationships upon which it depends must be built by intelligent people who are just as fanatically dedicated to their cause as their competitors.

The people you hire to take your brand to the top — whether in service of national security or simply trying to elbow the corner Starbucks out of business — absolutely must be empowered to win over each customer, one at a time.

Ideally you will have some sort of database supplementing their efforts as well, so that interactions with customers begin to be tracked and over time, you have a picture of each individual that is part of your unique business orbit.

Also ideally, you want to combine the customer relationship management system with a data mining system that tells you which of your customers is spending on what and how much, so you can isolate the highest value interactions and focus most of your time on those.

When that customer comes in, any person who is part of your team can tap into the program and then address them in the most unique, friendly and personalized terms, instead of numbly repeating the same nonsense words, over and over again, like a robot. Which only serves to infuriate customers, not to endear them to your brand.

Here's another example: Have you heard of the Jack Welch MBA Program? They advertised on LinkedIn and I inquired once. That was probably three months ago, and I have never followed up. But the person assigned to my original inquiry is still reaching out to me. And these aren't your standard-issue cookie-cutter emails, either. They're actually interesting, personalized letters that seem like they are specifically tailored to me, asking when I can talk, get assessed for my career goals, and develop an action plan that will move me, in my specific, particular snowflake career, forward.

I may never get an MBA in this lifetime. But you can bet your bottom dollar I'll always think of the Jack Welch program if and when I do decide to pursue one.

Now you may be thinking such personal attention is unrealistic. After all, brands can get very big, massively so. How can they actually converse as human beings with each individual customer? I am here to tell you that they absolutely can, and technology makes it more possible than ever, and that they have to.

The only thing getting in the way is attitude. If you as a business owner have the attitude that communication is your least important function versus "real things" like new product development and enhancement, you're screwed. If you favor "hard skills" because they're seemingly difficult to learn and require a lifetime of commitment by so-called "smart people," you're biased.

Emotional intelligence is hard to come by these days. The heart and soul of your brand always comes down to the person who interacts with the customer. Even if you operate an e-commerce business.

You say you value your customer service staff? Think about how little you are probably paying this person, how rarely or perfunctorily you are training them, how excessive the restriction you're placing on their interactions with the customer.

Do you make them say, before anything else: "I'm Jennifer, ID#5344, this conversation is recorded to ensure the highest possible level of customer service?"

That, my friend, is a "brandcuff!"

Do you really think a person suffocating under the weight of your condescending mistrust is going to provide a return on investment? Or maybe you think the only person who can build your brand is you — and possibly your highly paid, empowered and pampered senior management team.

Maybe it's time to rethink.

8

Why Federal Agency Branding Is Not Propaganda

Some people may think that branding a federal agency is, quite simply, not allowed. This is because we are strictly prohibited from engaging in propaganda—meaning any activity done simply for "self-aggrandizement" or "puffery" of the agency itself. And isn't that what brand-building is, simply the act of creating a well-known name?

Actually, no. Brand-building is about creating a very specific kind of relationship between an organization and its stakeholders, a relationship in which the stakeholders understand 1) that the organization exists 2) what an organization is promising to do for them and 3) what they must do in return to obtain goods or services from the organization (pay a fee, comply with specific rules, etc.). Ideally, to have strength, that relationship will be based on an image of the organization that is positive, high-level, and conceptually abstract—representing something more than just what the organization does on a day-to-day basis. For example, the Coast Guard arguably stands for "bravery," not

33

just "protecting the nation's waterways."

In a federal agency context, branding is accomplished through "disseminating information to the citizenry about the agency, its policies, practices, and products," a role for public affairs that is specifically allowed by the Government Accountability Office. (Branding is also accomplished through the actions of the agency itself, but the public affairs officer has no control over that except to try and explain those actions.)

People who think agencies shouldn't build a brand don't understand the distinction between brand-building as a process and a brand as an outcome. The process is about sharing information to help key stakeholders understand what the organization is about and how they should relate to it. The outcome is indeed a well-known name that is associated with certain promises.

(Now, there can be a very fine line between disseminating information about what an agency is and does for the sake of promoting positive compliance with agency rules, and promoting that agency's existence just for the sake of getting the public to be aware of the name. The difference has to do with intent.)

So far it may sound like agency branding begins and ends with citizen education initiatives. Yet this is far from the case, because the brand is shaped by all the communication that goes on about and around it. We can issue press releases on our website until we are blue in the face, but the fact of the matter is that the public is equally if not more influenced by others who are disseminating communication about us:

- The press writes about our rules and requirements as well

as any other story of interest to the public that concerns our agency;
- Congress will hold hearings about programs, events, and incidents that affect our agency; and
- The public will write about our communication and actions themselves, for example, in blogs and other social media vehicles such as Wikipedia.

All of those communications affect our brand because they affect the way the public understands and relates to us. So if we are to maintain a positive relationship with the public, in which the public understands who we are, what we do, and why we do it, we are responsible for engaging with all of these communicators to make sure that our message is clear. When we write op-eds in the press, respond to Congressional invitations to testify, and respond to citizen questions on our website, we are also branding the agency. Again, the end goal is to create and sustain a relationship with the public (not to mention our own employees) that is productive, leading to rules being followed with a sense of pride and enthusiasm for supporting the higher-level purpose of the agency.

If branding makes sense and is allowed, why does it seem to be in such short supply in the federal government? Perhaps this is due to the common, but misguided view that a public affairs officer's job is limited to simply supplying information about particular incidents, events, and programs without telling a broader story about what the agency is, why it exists, and how those incidents, events, and programs work together. It is important to tell the larger story in order to impress upon the public mind that the agency is a cohesive whole, and not just an assortment of individual sub-departments dealing with isolated incidents. It is possible that many federal public affairs officers shy away from creating that bigger picture because they don't want to be seen as promoting the agency for its own sake—that they are afraid of being seen as propagandizing.

The reality is, there are very few strong federal agency brands. And those brands that are strong—like the Coast Guard, the Secret Service, the FBI and the CIA—have become well-known not necessarily because of their public affairs offices, but because they have become visible through their extraordinary actions as portrayed in the news, on TV, and in the movies. For example, in the devastating aftermath of Hurricane Katrina in 2005, the Coast Guard rose to the rescue, with images of Coast Guard leadership saturating the media. And there have been many memorable portrayals of Secret Service, FBI and CIA agents in the movies and on TV.

Has anyone tried to build a federal agency brand from within a federal agency? No doubt many agencies are engaging in branding to some extent or another. But until we get rid of that dangerous misconception that branding is equivalent to propagandizing, they will likely encounter obstacles that prevent them from being fully successful.

The bottom line: for maximum effectiveness, federal agencies should engage in more than just providing information—they need to brand. Not for the sake of creating a name, but because it's the way to build the best possible relationship they can with the American people—increasing compliance with agency rules and demonstrating to the taxpayer that their dollars are being invested wisely.

9

Rebranding the Federal Workforce

Very simply, if the only reason to support federal employees is what could happen without us, then all you have to do is replace us with private sector contractors and see if the trains can still run on time.

Instead, the branding message for federal employees should focus on what makes us unique and irreplaceable. We have an amazing story to tell – why haven't we gone there yet? Why has nobody taken a positive approach?

If I could rebrand the federal workforce, I would take a three-pronged approach as follows:

- Address the negative stereotypes. They say we are lazy fat cats who live off the taxpayer's dime. We have to deal with that. (Renowned political strategist Dick Morris, who served as campaign manager and political adviser for former President Clinton, said recently on FOX News that Clinton told him, "Never let an attack go unanswered.") Responding means being accountable, because guess what? Sometimes "they" are right!

- Use "positioning" to show our unique value. "Position-ing" is a marketing tactic wherein you situate yourself as offering something that nobody else can. If you look at the characteristics of the very best federal employees – caring, versatile, resourceful, dedicated, generous, tough, educated, experienced, funny, diverse and gracious – I think we are doing ourselves tremendous harm by failing to tell our positive story. We do not need to subtly threaten the American public into taking care of us. We need only show concretely what we do, and how we contribute, the vast majority with good intentions.
- Portray a vision for the federal workforce that takes us one, five, ten years into the future. In my view the primary problem federal workers face right now is the fragmentation between agencies. What we don't seem to understand is that to the American public, we are ONE entity. In fact I would argue that they don't even see much difference between political employees and those in the civil service. We are all, together, "Washington." And we need to respond as one face with one voice.

In my view the single most powerful thing federal employees can do to rebrand ourselves – because it is us, it is our brand, and we are responsible for it – is to show how we absolutely kick a** as versus the private sector.

The federal employee must be seen as the very best that America has to offer.

We cannot brand our country with logos and labels and taglines and campaigns.

We can only brand our country through the faces and voices of the people who work for it. The people with whom the public interacts.

The asteroid that we Federal employees feared so much has landed: People are questioning our worth.

In response we have to get up and fight. Yes, it is time to compete for our own jobs.

Where we fall short we have to admit it – where we are doing well we cannot shy away from telling our own story.

There is no need to wait for some organization to do it for us. This is something that we can do for ourselves.

And because the American public really does count on us 24/7, recasting our identity collectively will be of great benefit to them, and to the stability of our country, as well.

10

The Whistleblower's Brand Paradox

Conventional communications advice is to "stay on message."

It is as if leaders have a script (wait, they do – it's called "talking points") and they're supposed to read from it. Like an actor in a play.

In real life things are not that simple. People don't believe uncritically anymore, if they ever did.

Today a leader's pronouncements are viewed as just another text to "deconstruct."

Resistance to and subversion of formal "messaging" takes place on a continuum from active to passive, for example:

- Investigative blogging
- Commentator blogging
- Tweeting or retweeting
- Posting on Facebook
- Recording a YouTube-type video of oneself voicing an opinion
- Taking a photograph

- Sharing a link directly from the Internet
- Forwarding an email containing a link

Not everybody in America is wealthy. But it doesn't take money to follow your conscience. Only a thinking mind, the ability to communicate, and access to a means of distributing one's sentiments.

Because Americans respect honest people, we connect with them, we tend to appreciate the fact that they speak out. Even when we disagree.

Therefore, promoting honest speech enhances the brand. Yet organizations continue not only to script leadership talk, but to punish the very whistleblowers whose honesty can build the organization's reputation if allegations are addressed.

Examples of such punishment are everywhere, including the front page of today's New York Times (June 18, 2012), an expose on the Albert M. "Bo" Robinson Assessment and Treatment Center in Trenton.

The worst thing about this halfway house isn't the poor conditions there. It is the allegation that workers knew about those poor conditions and reported them over and over again, only to be rebuffed – pressured to change their reports.

> *"Bronislaw Szulc, a former senior state official in charge of investigating conditions at halfway houses, said he had filed reams of reports....(he) said top officials in Trenton had often ignored his reports, rarely held the halfway houses' operators responsible and demanded that he soften his critical findings."*

Sometimes whistleblowers were even dismissed:

> *"Community Education soon fired several senior staff members at Bo Robinson, including Mr. Brumbaugh, the deputy security director and former correction officer, who had earned a reputation as a whistle-blower because he had highlighted problems there."*

I read a similar article in The Miami Herald just last week, "DJJ Watchdog Ousted After Criticizing Boss' Friend":

> *"Last week, Department of Juvenile Justice Secretary Wansley Walters informed Gov. Rick Scott that she intends to fire her agency's top watchdog. Inspector General Mary Roe Eubanks had held the job since 2004, and was a nearly 25-year state employee, with 10 years in state agency investigations. Eubanks was placed on administrative leave, with pay, while the termination was being approved."*

In the federal government as well, there is no shortage of employees speaking out about problems in the workplace, ranging from minor to major (GovLoop, Federal Soup, Cleanup ATF). It defies logic that people would place their livelihoods in jeopardy simply to report wrongdoing, especially when they haven't done anything wrong. They could look the other way and nobody would judge them badly.

But it's just the opposite. Over and over again, one runs into examples of people who put their careers and reputations on the line, only to do the right thing.

Sadly, when they do, it is often not the organization that

gets questioned, but the whistleblower. In fact, if persecuted, the whistleblower rapidly develops a personal brand – spelled t-r-o-u-b-l-e.

...Hold on a minute. If it's true that whistleblowers are immediately branded as "trouble," "muckrackers," "crazy," and so on, how can they be good for the organization's brand?

The answer has to do with contradictory survival instincts inside and outside the group.

- Inside: A critically thinking individual is disruptive because they resist the flow of "groupthink." Unless the organization is unusually self-reflective or under intense pressure to reform, it will favor those who "won't get in the way." Because most groups are dysfunctional. And indeed, as the famous Milgram study showed, they can find plenty of people who will go along with "whatever" when authority says "just do it" – even when it means they have to inflict incredible pain.
- Outside: Organizational stakeholders rely on the group or organization to be highly functional. They expect excellence and are inconvenienced by dysfunction. No kindergarten teacher can afford to make up for a parent's neglect; a community can't channel its faith through people who abuse the parishioners; citizens can't sit up at night worrying that police are in cahoots with organized criminals; we can't afford doctors who see elderly patients for five seconds then charge Medicare $250 for a full-fledged visit; and so on.

From a communications standpoint, the intractable problem is that what looks like "trouble" from inside the group – a whistleblower – is completely the opposite from an outside perspective.

Indeed, when whistleblowers step forward to tell the public what is going on – such as the brave girl in Scotland who photographed her lousy school lunch in an effort to get healthier food – the public applauds.

And they wait to see what the organization will do.

From a communication perspective the answer to this riddle is pretty simple. Organizations ought to build in robust reporting mechanisms for fraud, waste and abuse. Those mechanisms should be easy to access and easy to use. And they should provide for no reprisal (just the opposite, some kind of reward) for the whistleblower (assuming that person is not just engaging in malicious slander).

If wrongdoing is discovered internally first, the organization has an opportunity to investigate and fix it, then report transparently about these activities. It's a chance to prove that whatever trust it has, is warranted.

If wrongdoing leaks externally, the organization can claim the problem and again, investigate it, fix it, and report on it quickly, without undue delay. In a way that is just for all concerned.

A balanced reputation management like this – really, a form of brand management – allows the organization to put equivalent of money in the reputational bank. Capital that can be drawn on later, in the event of a crisis. Capital that can prevent good employees from leaving, and that can encourage them to turn in "bad apples" who sour a basically good organization to all.

It is unfortunate that this prescription – which I know I have seen in various forms before – has until now largely gone unheeded.

How many times will we have to see a "scandal" break in the news, when the simplest and most basic of reputation management programs would have prevented it in the first place. And would have kept incredibly valuable people engaged with, and passionate about, the organizations where they spend much of their waking time.

11

Authentic Branding In A Post-Branding World*

The key distinction between branding and post-branding is that people are looking for authenticity and the ultimate currency is trust.

Branding of course provides a partial view of the organization and is therefore prone to bad actors. Yet it is still possible to do this now. The key is to remember the distinction between branding and propaganda. Branding is a consistent approach to identity. Propaganda involves misleading people deliberately, or even outright lying. Don't propagandize.

Other tips:

- In a post-branded organization, the leader is the brand, not just endorsed by it.
- Focus on internal communication, start at the top, and let everyone build the brand.
- Treat frontline employees like human beings and live the brand as if it were their neighbor.
- Avoid "branded" writing and keep it plain.

46

- Avoid robotic language and use everyday, normal English.
- Coordinate logos and brand architecture to avoid distractions and maintain a cohesive brand.
- Deal with dissension by allowing people to express their dissent in an adult way, building buy-in and avoiding reprisals.
- Embrace social media and the web to support the younger generation and encourage group conversations.
- Enforcing existing policies on social media is essential, as is treating people like adults, including making them accountable for using good judgment.
- Training and employee buy-in are essential for supporting people in expressing the views of the organization in an educated, thoughtful way.

In summary, a strong agency's brand strategy should reflect its unique stakeholder relationships and services. To find and engage the audience, research their location and reach influencers. Engage with the representatives and provide context for their message. Avoid using templates as subject matter experts, as they are only guides to set expectations. Embrace culture and use line extensions sparingly to engage the public without diluting the original message.

Brands burn out when they don't evolve, so have at least one person on the team who refuses to "drink the Kool-Aid" and is allowed to tell it like it is. Branding is not a tool for creating publicity, but rather a long-term communication strategy that sets the foundation for marketing and PR.

Avoid using the B-word and focus on success in terms of executive wants. Address pain points in defining brand objectives and fix problems one at a time.

Note: AI was used to rewrite and edit the content for this article.

II

Career Development

12

5 Things You Should Know Before Joining The Federal Government

Culture, culture, culture – it's all about culture.

1. You never know who you're talking to. Quiet and unassuming people are routinely very powerful people. (It's bad form to be showy and self promotional.) So be extra careful to show everybody the same amount of respect.
2. You never know who is married to who, or in a relationship with who, or who has an archenemy where. Across four different agencies in ten years, I have learned to watch my step. Feds work in agencies for many years, find their partners there, get divorced there, and form bitter rivalries. Again, be careful what you say about who.
3. Everybody is confused by the amount of red tape. On a snow day like yesterday, we're all reading fifteen different guidances to make sure we know what to do. Never feel dumb about this. If you thought you knew the answers, we would be laughing at you.

4. Problems are usually worked out quietly, not in town halls. It's important to have events and send out corporate communications for the sake of making clear what priorities are. But real progress happens in small meetings where the microphones are off.

5. Every agency has its own culture, traditions and history and you need to know what you don't know. At one agency, you show up ten minutes late to a meeting and that's starting time. At another, attendance means coming five minutes early. Typically there are issues around field versus headquarters, or component versus headquarters, or division versus division. If you don't understand the sensitivities you can easily sound foolish

13

It's Not Too Late: Resolve to Have a Successful Year

Here are 10 tips for developing the attitude, intention and presentation that will help you reach your goals:

The Right Attitude

1. *Take yourself seriously.* Not seriously like in an egotistical way but seriously like your choices have consequences. If you aren't taking yourself seriously right now, I guarantee it has to do with the logic of depression, meaning that you tell yourself things like this: "I tried before, and I failed." If this is you, understand that your mind isn't functioning right. You're going to have to retrain your brain, even if you have to stand there in front of the bathroom mirror in the morning and make accurate statements to yourself repetitively. Not phony affirmations. Sentences such as this: "I can't control the past. I can control what I do right now."

2. *Stop being irrationally afraid.* Sometimes we think, "If X happens, I'm screwed." Sometimes we live our whole lives that way. We don't speak up when we should. We don't leave a bad job or a bad relationship. We don't break ties with toxic

friends, or family. Because we have this terrible cloud of fear hanging over us, an all-purpose sense of doom. Of course this isn't to tell you in some magical way that everything will be all right no matter what. It isn't to prescribe unrealistic choices. Sometimes you have to live with things you just don't like. But at the very least, you should say to yourself, "What is the worst thing that can happen if I act?" And then consciously decide to go one way or another. If you find that you are just paralyzed or consumed by fear, or anxious thoughts bubble up constantly, try writing the following sentence down, staring at it, saying it out loud (as above), and even putting it up on your bulletin board: "I am a survivor. I have survived a lot already. I am much stronger than I think."

3. *Surrender.* This is for the control freaks who can't prioritize, can't delegate, and can't take anything off their plate because they somehow think the weight of the world rests squarely on their shoulders. Don't believe in God? Just call it the Universe; do your best and then hit the "Let It Go" button.

4. *Be generous.* There is no rational reason to be nice to other people. Most of the time, they won't pay you back, and it's time you could have spent advancing your own self-interest. But somehow, when you give, the Universe does give back to you. It changes your mood and your attitude; it gives you a sense of purpose. That doesn't mean you should ignore your own needs, but it does mean that selflessness yields intangible dividends.

Intention Matters

5. *Adopt a posture of success.* If you can pick one thing to focus on, whether professional or personal, and then see that through, it will balance you. Remember it doesn't have to be

an outcome-based goal (lose 30 pounds); it can be a process-based goal (walk half an hour a day). The point is not really to achieve the goal, but rather to develop a genuine sense of belief in yourself.

6. Be accountable. We all know an excuse when other people use one, but it's all too easy to justify our own bad behavior. We avoid seeing things as they are and instead manipulate ourselves into believing that we are right, almost at any cost. How many arguments, how many accidents, how many crimes, how many lawsuits, and how many wars could be avoided if people simply asked: "That was a screwup on our end. How can we fix it?"

7. Pay attention to time. Make it a habit to be on time. This is not so much about the hands on the clock as it is about demonstrating respect for other people. It also forces you to be present at the meeting instead of thinking about other things or playing games with your cellphone. Similarly, keep an eye on how much of other people's time you are spending. Respect their need to get things done, and that time is very limited—it is the most valuable commodity on the planet.

Presentation Counts

8. Improve your verbal communication skills. I recently watched a video that had gone viral. It was amazing to me that the person featured on the video—essentially a spontaneous street confrontation—was so incredibly articulate, without any preparation or prompting. Regardless of your profession, regardless of your career level, and regardless of your educational achievements, you can impress people by demonstrating powerful rhetorical skills. If that seems like an overwhelming task, you can join a group like Toastmasters, which is specifically aimed at helping people improve their ability to speak in public. If you don't have the bandwidth or desire to take on yet another activity, a very simple way to start is by practicing with your cellphone. You can record yourself answering a question, and then view the video to see where you did well, and where you didn't.

9. *Dress better.* I did not say "dress well," or "dress expensively," or "dress in ways that are considered fashionable." Rather, I'm saying you should up your game, or in the words of Chef Emeril Lagasse: "Kick it up a notch." Your focus needs to be on things that are doable and authentic—you, only better. Believe me, people will notice.

10. *Improve your LinkedIn profile.* Here are two simple things you can do: 1) add two to three sentences under each job to explain what you did there (no typos!); and 2) you need recommendations. Not just endorsements, but actual words from people who know you and can say something nice. My personal preference is to reciprocate first, meaning go to a connection's page and recommend that person. To do this, click the down arrow next to "Send A Message," then click "Recommend." You can also ask directly for a recommendation—in person, by phone or by email. To do this, from your profile page, look underneath and to the right of your photo, where it says "View Profile As." Click the down arrow, then click "Ask To Be Recommended."

14

For a Successful Federal Career, You'll Need These 5 Things

Joining the federal government in 2003 was the cultural equivalent of sticking my finger into a light socket. It was a land where certain phrases — like "efficiency and effectiveness" — had almost magical inspirational powers. Anything that had those words in the mission statement was good; today the equivalent would be "innovation."

Back then, there were other words that were warning shots. Most notably "I have seniority here, get to the back of the line" — a command I had not heard in many years. If you are considering a career in the federal government, or if you already work there and want to be more successful, here are 5 crucial things to know about how the culture operates:

1. **Humility.** If you have been chosen to work for the federal government, you are one of the lucky ones, and you know it. You get to do work that is important for the country, you get paid a sustainable wage, and you work with nice and fair-minded people. So if you're egotistical, self-

promotional and ungrateful, you won't fit in very well.

2. **Sense of Humor.** Despite their somewhat serious exterior, feds — who typically have many years of experience at a single agency — have a long institutional memory and have seen innumerable cases of the wackiest stuff go down. There is almost nothing that surprises them, there is nothing new under the sun, and they have thus developed a Steven-Wright-like ability to make just about any crazy situation about a thousand pounds lighter with a laugh. Remember that no matter how much you know, you never can know too much — so enjoy being the person they tell all that "I can't believe it" stuff to on a daily basis.

3. **Detail Orientation.** In the federal government, employees are typically vastly overworked but also required to get things 100 percent right, not only in the substance but also in the process. Deadlines are shorter than ever, expectations are higher, but the constant drumbeat is that at some point you or your boss may be called upon to answer for your activities. The gold standard for any government employee is work that is "right" and also "right on time" — but if you have to choose between the two, accuracy always wins.

4. **Diplomacy.** In the federal government, the importance of consensus cannot be overstated. When someone has to make a big decision — a costly decision, a significant decision, one that affects a lot of lives — the best way to weigh the options is to err on the conservative side, ask a wide variety of experts for input, and take the route that has the least risk and the most benefits. As part of this system, if you're the kind of person who's

a lightning rod, who just always rubs people the wrong way, there will be folks who just don't want to deal with you. So cultivate the manners of a diplomat, so that you can email anyone and everyone, without causing aggravation.

5. **Integrity.** In any social institution, there will be bad actors. Dysfunction is routine in any organized grouping of people. That said, the headlines that emphasize bad behavior are in my experience very distorted. Government employees are all about doing the right thing, and when there's even a whiff of breaking the rules they will point that out and do it loudly. Some people are more diplomatic at pointing out potential problems than others; as a friend once said, "you must learn the gift of sharing just the options and the risks, with no opinions."

So those are my tips for success in the federal government: Be humble and of good humor; be accurate and treat people respectfully; and honor the position of trust that you've been given. All those things together make for someone whose presence is truly prized.

15

How To Become Compulsively Successful

Project management sucks. Anyone who's spent five minutes in a large organization knows this. But there are people who manage to get it done: on time, on budget, high quality. And it's not only because of the conventional wisdom about what we can rely on to make a project great:

It's not about automation tools. They don't tout Trello, brag about Basecamp, or insist that "Sharepoint really works, if you take the time to learn it."

It's not about PM certification. I've seen highly trained PMs mouth off and melt down, just like there are those who get done without ever having cracked a textbook. Regular, agile, waterfall, windmill...none of it makes a difference.

It's not about communication, or emotional intelligence. That helps, of course, but I've seen virtual robots in human form power-saw through projects without so much as saying "good morning."

Here is what the best project managers have: An intensely powerful compulsion to fashion order out of chaos. You might think that such people would go for peaceful careers, like . . . I don't know, marine biologist? But it's just the opposite. They unconsciously gravitate toward fixing disarray.Think about it: Who else could deal with demoralized teams; fuzzy or constantly morphing requirements; out-of-control costs; finger-pointing partners; and hellish, endless, migraine-inducing meetings? Only someone who gets a more-than-the-paycheck sense of accomplishment by bringing things under control. Want to pick out a good PM in a crowd? Look for:

- Statements like this: "I'm not gonna live in the land of crazy," and "chaos doesn't work for me."
- Myers-Briggs type INTJ: sees the big picture, "gets" what's going on, calls people out, visibly irritated by those who go off-track.
- Insistence on documentation: These people don't do "handshake deals." There is a project charter, a calendar in hard-copy, meeting agendas and minutes, and recorded approvals. Every time.

Why does the compulsion to PM matter? Because the same principle holds true across careers. You will excel at whatever you're driven to do. I know a person who's obsessed with special effects makeup. Every time I go to the drugstore, she stops to show me her latest "puncture wound" photo. Another takes seventeen selfies a day. And posts them! A third person must be liked by everyone. A fourth has the compulsion to manipulate. A fifth "eats clean" - always talking up some natural remedy that will "remove all the toxins from your gut."

Most of the time we think of these compulsions as "bad." We tell people to go for therapy, talk it out, and live a more balanced life. But what if we reframed unconscious inner drives, and focused only on ways to harness them positively?

What is a brand, if not a driving obsession? From this perspective, talent acquisition is more than just deciphering what people can naturally do. It's also about learning what they must do, what they are driven to do, for reasons neither of you will probably ever know, understand or control.

16

One Solid Way to Fail, But Not Fall, in 2016

I was thinking about the pressure we're all under walking back into the office after New Year's.

Vacation is over, the resolutions are made and it feels like there are just so many of them: "Eat clean," "learn to construct a computer," "get my college degree," even "work hard and get that promotion."

But as we all know, trying to do too many things, or making theoretical commitments without an actual plan for implementation, is only a recipe for failure. So perhaps it is wiser to make just one resolution you can keep.

If you're thinking about making a professional change for the better, you might want to consider this paradox: Some employees make a lot of mistakes but don't seem to suffer any consequences, while others seem to land in hot water for the slightest infraction.

After more than two decades of observing workplace inter-action and reading about same for work and for pleasure, I think I have pinpointed what makes the crucial difference.

If you master this skill, in small increments over time, you will see a positive impact on your career. I call it "the Zelig principle."

Briefly, Zelig was the main character in a 1983 Woody Allen movie of the same name. He had a personality a lot like tofu: Whatever strong personality was around, like a sauce, that was the flavor he took on.

Am I saying that you should sell out and be self-effacing? Totally not. But it does make sense to tone it down at work, if you seriously want to supersede 2015.

Of course, this is much easier to say than to do. At work, like at home or in any social arena, there will be some people you have a good personality chemistry with, while there are others you repel almost chemically. It almost seems beyond one's control to accomplish.

However, there are a few things you can do to put the odds more in your favor. The below are based on my personal observation and experience, and will probably echo much of what you've already heard:

- Have the right attitude
- Focus on other people's feelings
- Follow the social norms of the workplace
- Deliver excellent work
- Give the credit to your boss and teammates

If you read this list carefully, none of it involves being a phony. You don't have to dress like the boss, mimic his or her mannerisms, or become known as a flaming kiss-up.

Really it's about evolving yourself.

Childhood is about indoctrination to the identity of our

parents. Adulthood is the process of breaking free and finding out who you are as opposed to what they told you.

Maturity is the capacity to focus on the self of others.

At work, the employee who exhibits the qualities of maturity has the greatest prospects of success. This person will make mistakes just like anyone, but the positive self-esteem s/he provides to everybody else acts like a buffer against the harshness of their judgments.

We shouldn't promote or condone incompetence; that's corruption. But it's very legitimate to support a culture of maturity at work. And it's a personally valuable decision when we decide to evolve our personalities, to consistently preserve the dignity of others.

17

5 Things About Work You Have to Get Used to

Reality:

1.It's not supposed to be "fun." In fact, work is the opposite of "fun." That's because somebody else is paying you to do it. If you were paying yourself, you would make it fun — of course. But you aren't the boss. So deal with it.

2. Nobody has to help you. When you go to work, it is your job to figure things out. It is not the job of your boss to figure things out for you. Nor is it the job of your teammates, HR, the training department, or anybody else in the orbit of the parking lot. It's you.

3. Somebody doesn't like you. Yes I know you try really hard to be very nice and helpful and to get along. Guess what? It doesn't work. At least not with everyone. There is something about you that really, really, really rubs at least one person around you very much the wrong way. And that will never change, unless you leave and they forget you ever existed. And even then the mere mention of your name will cause their eyebrows to furrow deeply in annoyance.

4. It's all about competition. You read online that it's a "collaboration economy," and of course to an extent that is true. But people do not collaborate with you because they want to help you win. They help you out because there's something in it for them. And if they could elbow you out and take the spoils of your job and your benefits for themselves — that is called the career ladder, and they absolutely, positively would.

5. You succeed by serving your boss. I know you graduated from a really good school at the top of your class, and you can make an app, and you're really well-prepared and read *everything you can* about the organization, its space and your expertise. But I hate to tell you, if you come in every day with a self-important, arrogant attitude, your days are numbered in that organization of yours, and you will be replaced before you can even utter the words "you'll be sorry." Everyone is replaceable, and you stay employed by doing what it is your boss needs done.

18

The Evolution Of Professional Self On Social Media

Here are two facts about life in 2015 that you may or may not like, depending on your familiarity with and attitudes toward social media. And your beliefs about what the term "professional" means.

The first is that you are you, always you, no matter where you are. There you are on Instagram, on Pinterest, on Twitter, on LinkedIn, on Facebook and Reddit. You are there in the comments, you are there in your vacation pics and the memes you repost. The news stories you share and the comments you like, oh the comments.

People get to know you as an amalgam of all of these things. And while your quirky personality may have been a professional liability five years ago, it is a tremendous asset now. You should absolutely be yourself, and the more you are yourself the happier you'll be as well as the more employable.

The second is that social media is more and more realizing its capacity as the ultimate crowdsourcing tool for reason. By that I mean, information that is useful will bubble up to the top. If it is logical, helpful, rational it will rise. If it is emotionally raw in an engaging and meaningful way it will rise. If it brings people together it will also rise. On the other hand if it's irrational ranting and raving, propaganda and hate, or if it's self-indulgent trash, it will sink.

Nowadays people look you up online. You have no choice, really, but to be yourself.

19

Do Government Employees Have Freedom Of Speech?

It's a free country, everybody has freedom of speech, and it is statistically impossible that you will agree with every single thing your agency, another agency or the government does as a whole.

You want to make the government work better. And every day people take to social media, face-to-face conversation and everything in between to say what they think.

Plus, honest conversation promotes transparency and therefore credibility. To my mind it shows the public that we care.

However, there are times when speaking your mind may not be the best choice.

Here are five factors I use to guide and sometimes limit my public comments:

- Focus on the general (rules and best practices) not the specific.
- Remember that I am in a sense a representative of my

Agency's brand (and the brand of government) whether I am speaking in a personal capacity or not. This is true of any employee of any organization.

- Stick to designated roles and responsibilities – in my Agency only Public Affairs or designated experts on specific topics are authorized to explain or comment on what we do publicly, and to address controversy.
- Do not do anything that may interfere with mission performance. In some Agencies this is written into a code of conduct.
- Confidentiality–don't talk about things that are nonpublic information.

Since then: a few updates that can all be boiled down to "good judgment":

- There is no foolproof decision filter for any of this; the answer is often "it depends."
- Given the low trust that the public has in government, I actually think it reinforces government credibility when employees themselves are respectfully critical.
- There are going to be times that all of us go out on a limb because of an issue we care about. We should never be so cautious and so guarded that we forget to be human, as long as we are appropriate, constructive and follow the law. One good middle of the road approach is to focus, rather than taking on everything. Another is to limit the audience for your past personal posts as they become irrelevant.
- Social media is increasingly making it impossible to distinguish professional from personal, and we are really

going to have to think through the norms that will dually make us trustworthy in a social media setting while also maintaining a distinct public persona as a civil servant – this is a very complicated row to hoe.

- It is always important to choose your words carefully, and also to remember that whether you intend it or not, or have a disclaimer or not, if you are known as a federal employee then you may be seen as speaking on behalf of the government. This is particularly so if you inhabit a visible position, a high ranking position, or a position where you engage in outreach on the same platform where you speak in a personal capacity.

I am a deep believer in our civil right to freedom of speech and in my mind and heart I know it ultimately moves us forward. At the same time, I am also a believer that when you work for any organization you are ethically bound not to get in the way of its operations. And we do live in the real world, a world where social media has effectively erased the line between professional and personal.

In my view, the ideal balance is to present yourself always authentically, but diplomatically.

Everyone feels strongly about things. You don't want to seem like the kind of person who's forever hiding, but you also don't want to make it impossible for others to work with you.

III

Civil Service

20

Time to Establish a Centralized Federal Office Dedicated to the Communication Function

Imagine if the federal government employed pilots who couldn't fly. Doctors that couldn't do surgery. Lawyers who couldn't analyze a case. Budget analysts who couldn't add. Computer scientists who couldn't read code. Criminal investigators who could not track a suspect. And so on.

What would happen to the troops overseas absent intelligence analysts at home?

Yet we have no problem with obvious communication blunders on the part of the Federal government. The reason of course is that we do not see the financial cost of poor communication right away, or in a tangible way. But of course they are there. For example:

- Waste, fraud and abuse: Due to duplicative outreach by multiple agencies, i.e. human trafficking campaigns. Due to allowing agencies to buy unnecessary outreach services. Due to excessive reliance on vendors for web design and failure to manage their implementation, as occurred with the launch of the Obamacare system. Of course poorly conceived outreach campaigns and badly designed websites create a situation where thieves can lure the public into paying for what is already free, or giving away information on a copycat website.

· Unmotivated employees, retraining costs, loss of institutional knowledge, and high recruitment costs: Due to a ignoring federal employees as an audience – not only an audience of each individual agency. Due to a systemic lack of upward feedback channels and the threat of retaliation for whistleblowing. Due to a fundamental lack of understanding about what promotes good morale and what doesn't – for example the ATF's recent decision blocking a manuscript on "Fast and Furious." The opposition itself is going to generate a lot of press, which is going to make them look bad, and cause the media to re-visit a scandal dealt with years ago.

· Anti-government sentiment and possibly failure to comply with the law: Due to the failure of government communicators to proactively or defensively respond in crisis situations. Consider the bumbling responses to Edward Snowden's theft of information from NSA, the " incompetence, not malice" Benghazi defense; Kathleen Sebelius' poor performance on the Jon Stewart show regarding Obamacare, leading his calling her a liar. Lack of a plausible explanation for the Department of Justice Associated Press investigation led Watergate reporter Carl Bernstein to excoriate this. Recently, *New York Times* reporter David Sanger called the current Administration "the most closed, closed, control-freak I've ever encountered."

The preacher Joel Osteen says "don't bring a problem to your boss without also bringing a solution." I work for the federal government, so here is a suggestion: Set up an Office of Federal Communications within her purview. It would be situated alongside the Offices of Federal Financial Management; Federal Procurement Policy; E-Government and Information Technology; Performance and Personnel Management; and Information and Regulatory Affairs.

This Office would save money by eliminating duplicate work by individual agencies and it would be funded by the agencies where the money was saved. It would:

1. Serve as a liaison between the White House and federal agencies, coordinating official communications internally and externally.
2. Establish a governmentwide brand council overseeing communications from visual coordination to standardized content. This would include standard templates and elements for government communication to ensure consistency and comprehensiveness.
3. Establish governmentwide structures, guidelines, and ethics rules for federal agency communication including public affairs, information dissemination, websites, social media, mobile and other forms of new media.
4. Establish a government speakers' council where any subject matter expert in any agency can sign up to learn how to communicate effectively in the media, and can then be free to explain agency activities within the

bounds specified by governmentwide rules.

5. Establish a mechanism to review outreach contracts per agency above a certain threshold for signs of waste, fraud and abuse and to discover possible means of consolidation with other agencies.

6. Stand up a governmentwide customer service center to include service by email, chat, and telephone staffed by representatives from individual agencies but managed by a single source.

7. Centralize and manage open data posting and accessibility via the Web.

8. Establish the Federal Communication Training Institute, dedicated to enhancing employee skills and ensuring that people representing the government meet qualifying standards.

9. Establish a governmentwide Internal Communications Network within which employees can form a broad social network, communicate and collaborate simply and effectively.

10. Formalize the Federal Communicators Network as a network of Agency communicators represented in the Office so that decisions can be coordinated at the Agency level and customized in a way that makes sense for each particular mission.

Communication is a fundamental management activity. And yet communication is ignored in a fundamental, systemic, proactive way. A recent poll stated that less than half of Americans, 49% (an "all time low") think the government is capable of handling problems.

If we really want to serve the public well, prepare for

unforeseen crises, and reduce unnecessary spending at the same time, we should stop ignoring the hidden costs of communication incompetence by the government. And set a goal of increasing public confidence in our reliability to at least 75%.

21

10 Ways To Empower Government Employees

Public servants have faced the threat of a government shut-down more than once. Though fortunately these were averted, the sensation of having your head on a chopping block (even if temporary) can leave you unsettled and afraid. But we can empower government employees to have more control over their (our) own fates by implementing some structural changes that would promote and reward for productivity and efficiency — facilitating effective government from the inside out.

A few areas where we can do this in a low-cost, high-impact way:

Mentoring: Times are changing quickly and employees need to learn to adapt their skills accordingly. An on-the-job buddy at a higher level can be an invaluable asset in retaining good employees and helping them learn the often-subtle skills they need to contribute effectively. And it doesn't cost anything other than time.

Technology training: People who do things the old way

when there are faster, cheaper, better ways to get the job done may be comfortable, but also wasting taxpayer money and their own opportunity to grow professionally. Let this be the year we learn how to use technology. Again, it doesn't have to cost a cent if you get skilled employees to teach those who are just learning.

Performance planning: An employee's performance plan for the year should be a guiding document that they generate to align with agency and office goals. It should not be up to a manager to tell someone how they fit in, but rather this is a chance for a person to learn more about the mission and where they belong. It's also a chance to re-orient once a year and make sure the scope of one's position is of value. Worst comes to worst, a person needs to be reassigned, but that is a realization best made by the employee.

Evaluations: Here again, allow the employee to evaluate themselves, and bolster that with a 360 degree evaluation from a panel of supervisor and peers. It doesn't have to be lengthy or complicated, but it should be a combination of numerical ratings and narrative content so that a person receives a truer picture of how they've done and where they can improve in the next year. The more engaged the employee is in evaluating themselves, the more it will mean to them and the more it will be a true process for both them and their supervisors.

Rotations: Many people in government have served for decades. They have experience that cannot be learned in college and that cannot be easily duplicated. After many years in one place, it would be of benefit for them to rotate to other agencies, preferably of their choosing, learn new skills, and offer back some of their accumulated wisdom in return.

New experiences keep people fresh and mindful that we all ultimately work for one government, not just an assortment of agencies.

Retraining: When someone is no longer adding sufficient value in the position they hold, retrain them. It's not a shameful thing to admit that skills you had 30 years ago might not be as useful today, and that some adaptation is needed. Again, the better your skills the better your resume, so if the government is willing to assist an employee in retraining rather than let them flap around uselessly, that is a wonderful and empowering option for them to take. And it need not cost anything other than on-the-job training.

Communities of interest: If you have a group of thousands of people doing the same kind of work (e.g. writing), it makes sense to connect them in person or virtually so that they can support one another. Peer networks encourage excellence from within.

Interagency councils: These are groups of government employees that work across agencies on a formal or informal basis to consult on best practices, make recommendations, and generally leverage employee insights to help government move forward on matters of interest. There are a number of good examples in the government already and it seems we could expand on this greatly if employees were encouraged to do so.

Work/life self-help and fitness groups: I have noticed that federal employees love groups like Toastmasters, Weight Watchers, and even spiritually oriented groups that gather once a week for a lunchtime break focused on personal growth. It is a good thing for government to encourage employees to take advantage of these, as they increase skills, increase fitness, and teach employees to take responsibility for fixing problems on their own if possible.

Charity and volunteering: There is no better feeling when you're down than that of helping someone else. If government employees - who are public servants, in the end - are encouraged to do even more charity and volunteer work than they already do, it would lift spirits and build excellent relationships between government and the public, which add to the trust reserve that enables good government.

IV

Customer Service

22

What Government Can Learn From Apple Customer Service

To hear the horror stories circulating on Facebook, on some days it seems that everybody hates calling customer service.

CustomerThink's Brian Smith rattles off the laundry list of annoyances:

- Waiting too long.
- Repeating the same information over and over again.
- Representatives who don't know what they're talking about.

Of course, let's not forget the representative who sounds "robotic," like they are reading off a script. It turns out 40 percent of respondents to a recent survey hate that too, reports Michele McGovern at CustomerExperienceInsight.com — even though 60 percent of us still prefer to pick up the phone when it's time to ask for help.

We Get This in Government All the Time

As a government employee, I've been on the receiving end

of those frantic calls. The customer is always frustrated, sometimes beyond belief. They've called and emailed and Googled for the information 20 ways to Sunday, but somehow they just cannot get through to the right person.

I've even seen companies offer, for a fee, to help customers get the government customer service that is actually perfectly free. This has nothing to do with any required payments and everything to do with the fact that the government's way of providing the customer with information can be very dense and even impossible to understand.

Branding: The Missing Link

Part of the problem with customer service is that many organizations, government agencies included, do not under-stand what customer service is or means or how it relates to the brand at all.

To the average person, which is to say the average executive unschooled in the vagaries of customer service, you can reduce the entire equation briefly to the Staples "easy" button, and they love to say, over and over again, "That was easy! Just make it like that!"

But dealing with customers effectively is not just about making it "easy" and "quick." It's actually about emotional labor as well, a concept first proposed by sociologist Arlie Hochschild in 1983, in her classic book *The Managed Heart*.

That 'Special Friend'

The bottom line is that today, for a variety of reasons — and you may think them silly, but the customer is the customer is the customer — people expect an interaction with customer service to be as rewarding as a conversation with a friend.

Lest you say that brand has nothing to do with this because "all good customer service experiences are alike," the reality is that people also expect every customer experience to be deeply reflective of the brand. Almost as if the brand were a certain friend as distinct from somebody else.

When you go to the Four Seasons hotel, they wait on you well beyond what normal waiting on hand and foot is. It is recognizable as "The Four Seasons Way." If I had the money to do it, I would never stay anywhere else.

When you shop for food at Trader Joe's, every employee is called a "crew member" and part of their job is to give you that "yo ho ho," "all aboard" "ahoy" type of experience at the cash register. They play '80s music on the sound system constantly. Their attitude is "let's get it done," "we're all excited to be chipping in and helping you find and enjoy your food." Again, if I have a choice, I do not shop for food anywhere else.

But rarely do I have a good *and branded* experience with telephone (or chat) customer service. So when that happened today, with Apple, I made note of every single thing that worked. Because the entire interaction not only corrects the typical deficiencies of customer service, it would not have been possible without it being shaped by the values of the brand: passion, user delight, simplicity and more.

Valuing Brand Values

Steve Jobs knew the importance of brand values many years before it was "hot" to integrate them with marketing. Here is a speech in which he talked about it, noting that values are not only important but a key differentiator for the company in the eyes of the customer.

"Our customers want to know who is Apple and what is it we stand for. Where do we fit in this world? . . . Apple at the core, its core value, is that we believe that people with passion CAN

change the world for the better. That's what we believe." — *Steve Jobs*

Values are so much a part of the Apple culture that they rise to the level of implicit knowledge — embedded everywhere, without needing to be spoken aloud.

Korhan Buyukdemirci, service design lead at Motley Agency, attempted to articulate its set of core values clearly, noting that they are very similar to those of Google. (Which is OK — the same values can be shared by two different companies and expressed in customer service in very different ways.)

What Apple has done is take the key elements of customer service excellence and wrap them in the brand, in an efficient and automated way, without anyone acting like a robot in the process.

Today's Interaction: A Case In Point

The first thing you notice is the people. The same nice, helpful, Apple-dressed individuals you see on the "Contact Us" page stay with you through the whole process. (And, of course, they are dressed the very same way in the stores.)

After clicking a few simple screens, within less than 2 minutes I had a chat going. Sure I would have preferred to make a phone call to a human being, but I could also understand that Apple has a high-volume business, and that a chat fits in with simplicity, automation, being efficient.

Nevertheless, I steeled myself for a frustrating, miserable, irritating and prolonged experience. I've had them with other brands.

To my absolute surprise, the entire encounter was just the opposite. It was perfection. Quickly I was connected to a rep who took responsibility for the contact, identifying himself by name and getting my information for me.

Also immediately, I was provided a phone number to call and a URL to click just in case we got disconnected. And then the customer service representative called me by my first name and asked how I am doing.

Obviously, of course, this is all from a script. But the way Apple did it, none of it felt scripted.

I vented my frustration to the rep.

Right there was the empathy — which is just as important as solving the problem.

A little bit more interchange, and I got a full answer to my question. In addition to that, the rep solved another problem which would otherwise have required a separate call.

None of This Is Rocket Science

Of course, all this is basic common sense. But it is complicated common sense. Apple, for example, has a certain kind of "voice" that was evident in the call and remained consistent throughout. The rep somehow followed a set of rules but also made the dialogue seem spontaneous — and inserted mention of the brand repeatedly along the way.

The contact closed out with the usual "if there are no further questions," but again with a branded twist. Instead of just "hanging up," there was that little green checkmark. It told me that things were officially resolved, good and positive — and now I could go about the rest of my day.

'Small Things' Matter Big Time

That icon might seem minor, but it functions like a "visual hammer," as brand strategist Laura Ries puts it. To put it simply, this tool creates an association in my mind between a brand and a feeling, and every time I see it that connection is reinforced.

The Lesson for Government

Of course, the government isn't actually selling anything.

But it is — most importantly, it is marketing itself to the public as a repository of trust.

And so the government can and should do many things to up its customer service game to Apple-like standards. Both survey results and anecdotal evidence from family and friends confirms to me that although people deeply distrust the government, they have very strong positive feelings toward government employees.

So it is a very short step for federal agencies to combine three things to achieve branded customer service excellence:

- **Automated systems with deep reservoirs of data** that can intelligently analyze customers' problems quickly and get them the personalized answers they need.
- **Scripts for customer service that emphasize the unique mission of the agency** and the appropriate tone of voice and attitude given that mission. (For example, a representative from the FBI should sound different than one from Social Security.)
- **Visual icons beyond the standard logo** that reinforce the persona of the agency in the customer's mind — both with uniformed employees and with icons.

How Can You Lose?

Branded customer service, done well, offers an endless upside. With a single investment, the government can:

- **Promote the general "good government" goal of a happy populace** — or at least, a less frustrated one.
- **Reverse the perception that "the government doesn't**

know what it's doing."
- **Eliminate hucksters from the equation,** who profit off the weak and vulnerable, by helping the public know where to go for authentic and free information.
- **Deposit "money" in the bank account of future trust,** which is needed when a crisis hits.
- **Mitigate the risk of a future crisis** if and when the public needs to turn to the government for help in great numbers, such as in a time of disaster.

The principles of branding customer service are important for the private sector. Most organizations haven't mastered them. They should, as a critical company differentiator.

The government should take a leap in this direction as well. As uncomfortable as it may be to speak in "private sector language," getting on the level of the customer is critical. For no matter how much we like to poke fun and complain, all of us need it to function, and function well.

V

Communication

23

We Need A Plan for Federal Communications

As a government communicator I have always had a heightened sensitivity to the gap between what the public wants to hear and what the government wants to say.

I've also understood that the government tends to play catch-up with the communication tools used by the private sector. (It took us years to legitimize the use of social media.)

In 2016-2017 one of my major labors of love was a research paper called "Advancing Federal Communications." Dozens of us worked on this paper. It called for professional standards for federal communications, similar to the concept used in the UK.

There, the government releases an annual plan for government communication outlining its priorities.

When it comes to communication, the UK also explicitly values measurement, what we might call evaluation.

We all know that in the United States, trust in government is at or near historic lows. We can speculate as to why that is. No doubt performance is a significant part of it.

But so is communication.

When I started working for the government in 2003, the preferred communication style was excessively technical. Nobody could understand what we were talking about. Subject matter experts ruled.

Landmark: President Obama signed the 2010 Plain Writing Act requiring that federal agencies use clear government communication that the public can understand and use.

But problems remain.

Somebody very smart recently was asked what they would do to improve the function of an organization. That person said, let's talk about enhancing the quality of what's already there—not knocking people down. I agree with that approach.

So let's be positive, and talk about what government communicators tend to have in common: dedication, smarts, nuanced thinking, clarity of writing, technical skill. Let's build on that.

At a higher level, government communicators also tend to be good at offering strategic, nonpartisan advice.

But federal communicators often don't have a seat at the table where communication decisions are made. (Even if they're literally, physically in the room, objective advice is often not wanted.)

They are not taken seriously. And the reason for this, I believe, is a lack of standards for the profession. For example, project management has the Project Management Body of Knowledge (PMBOK), and related certification.

Government communicators don't even have a single unifying definition of "communication." Furthermore, there is no bachelor's degree in the civil service that I am aware of. There is no major concentration in "federal government communications." There isn't even a guidebook that tells people what legal and regulatory authorities they're following as government communicators.

You wouldn't go on Shark Tank without a business plan. Similarly the government cannot magically operate communications without a strategic communication plan for the employees who conduct outreach or convey information.

This really has nothing to do with politics, and it shouldn't. Government communication needs to be nonpartisan.

The only way for a body of work to avoid being dragged into ideology wars is for the work to adhere to a set of professional standards. You should be able to audit government communication accordingly.

Unfortunately, most of what the government has in the way of standards for communicators can be reducible to "thou shalt not," as in "thou shalt not engage in propaganda, puffery, or grassroots lobbying."

While it's helpful to know what NOT to do, this doesn't exactly tell us what TO do. We know that communication is an affirmative duty to ensure accountability and compliance, but that's about it.

There are multiple ways to tackle the situation, but first and foremost there has to be motivation at the highest levels to tackle it. (Not only among communicators themselves.)

Here's hoping that the future will bring us an institutional structure dedicated to establishing standards and annual plans for government communication. Those should clearly establish what the public can expect and how they can complain, and obtain recourse, if they don't get it.

Here's hoping that the government will use its communicators to the fullest, to share as much information as we can, as accurately as we can, as clearly as we can, to ensure the most accountability and compliance possible.

24

The 5 Nuts & Bolts of Operational Communication

A long time ago I had a boss who compared branding to the game of dominos. Also to a light switch. At the same time.

If you are into branding you know that it soaks into your mind. It's like trying to wash red Kool-Aid out of a white ceramic mug. Impossible.

So the boss was talking, and of course you are not going to disagree with your boss, unless they say something totally nuts or offensive. He said:

"Branding is like a light switch that goes off in your head. Until you get it, you don't get it."

Yep, yep, yep. Dilbert me. Absolutely.

"And then once that light switch goes off, it's like the dominos keep falling. You want everything to be branded, and everything to fall into place."

I did not really see my own rose-tinted glasses until a few months ago, when I changed positions to lead communications for a large, complex, technical and operationally focused division of a government agency.

Here are 5 things I've learned:

- 1) Communication is a support function (!), not the center of the universe. You forget this when you work in public affairs, or in a branding consultancy, because you and your peers are constantly arguing over "what is a brand" or "will social media eclipse print?" First of all this means – learn the business because you probably already know enough technique. Second of all it means – do.not.bother.busy.people.
- 2) Writing still matters. Grammar counts. Consistency is valued. Templates are beloved. Clean, clear, crisp text is adored. It's nice that not every corner of the Earth has been replaced by texts, tweets and status updates. Concise is good but specificity is just as important.
- 3) Talking is not considered "communicating." (Yes I know it actually IS communicating, but this is about perception.) Do you want to improve the quality of face-to-face communication, group interaction, culture and meetings? Get a degree in organizational development. Become a consultant so that you can lead retreats.
- 4) Social media is largely beside the point. If you are dazzled by all the gizmos and gadgetry associated with digital design you will be bored because operational peo-ple need practical skills. Project management. Process reengineering. Knowledge management. Collaboration sites. Portals. How to sort the wheat of information from the chaff that is most data. The production, organization, and retrieval of quality information. Believe it or not, it is an art form and it is hugely in demand.
- 5) Branding is only a byproduct. This last part is what

really astonished me. Much of the conversation in the communication world has to do with persuasion. What's the right tool to create awareness, engagement, loyalty, conversion to purchase (or membership or voting), etc. Often the "what" (the substance) is buried beneath messaging to the point where the original meaning almost gets lost. This kind of talk, which most of us would recognize as brand communication, is 70-80% useless in an operational environment. There, the desire is for factual information conveyed just-in-time.

In an operational world, it's not that there is no connection between words and brand. However, the typical equation that we see nowadays is reversed: it's substance first, decoration later.

Sometimes the creative part can take precedence. On "Inside the Actors Studio," Johnny Depp said that when he used to write songs, he wrote the music first and the words later. On the same show Robert Downey, Jr. said that the '80s director John Hughes used to write the movie according to the soundtrack. (Look how well they've done.)

But in an operational environment, the soundtrack comes last. And that's the way it should be.

25

The No. 1 Reason Why Your Presentation Sucks

For some people, public speaking is more terrifying than death. If that's you, the reason for this is the same as why your presentations are probably terrible.

It's not that you don't know your subject matter. You likely know it better than the back of your hand.

It's not that you aren't prepared, either. Most likely you've not only studied-up, but probably spent a little too much time hitting the books before your big Ted Talk or senior briefing.

The truth is that while some of us are naturally more theatrical than others, presentation skills can be learned.

So why are you so bad at public speaking? Why is your audience changing the channel, at least mentally, for 99 percent of your talk?

The issue is a basic flaw in your thinking. Please, rinse and repeat the following four words: *It's not about me.* Say it again: *It's not about me.*

If you get up there thinking about yourself, I can tell you right now: your talk will have zero impact. Or worse.

The reason great speakers affect us so much is that they are totally swept up in the power of their message.

It is impossible to focus on yourself and also put the spotlight on a topic that matters.

Fear of public speaking is a sign that you're definitely making this mistake. Your negative emotional investment is a gigantic red flag, signaling that your talk is wrapped around your ego.

The next time you have to give a talk, subtract yourself from the equation. You can prepare to do this in a very simple way—start doing videos. You don't have to publish them on YouTube or Periscope or anywhere else. You should, however, practice the art of speaking into the camera, on a regular basis, and then play back the video, to see what you look like while talking.

The point is not to evaluate your performance as a speaker. It's also not to gauge whether you know what you're talking about. Rather, it's about getting used to the fact that you actually look pretty bad on video.

Once you accept and get over that fact, and also manage to swallow your many flaws as a speaker, you'll get past your preoccupation with self altogether.

The truth is that the thing you fear the most is actually very real. You aren't all that good, you have a million flaws, and when you stand up there people know it.

It's ceasing to care that allows you to focus on the topic at hand. I happen to have a big nose. It used to embarrass me and I seriously considered a nose job. Now I like to laugh. That's me, that's my schnozz, that's the sun dancing off my wrinkles. It's okay to go gray and to grow a potbelly, too.

What people really do care about is the beating heart inside you. Good intentions, married with clear thinking, is what carries society forward.

Our most pro-social instincts go to work when we see you on stage. Get over your ego and put your message out front.

26

Tell It To Me Like I'm Stupid

"OK, let's get him on the phone."

That's radio talk show host Kane. It's the 99.5 FM radio segment "War of the Roses," it plays around 8 a.m. on weekdays, and it's really fun to listen to him and Intern John catch cheaters in the act.

In the script, Kane plays a guy who owns a flower shop.

"Hello, my name is ______, I'm calling from ___ Flowers. Is Pete there?"

"This is Pete."

"We're doing a promotion today, just for picking up the phone, you get a bouquet of roses sent to anyone of your choice."

"Who is this?"

"We're your local friendly flower shop, just trying to drum up some local business and compete with the big boys, y'now?"

"How did you get this number?"

"We subscribe to all the local customer lists."

(Sounding confused) "Oh."

"So who should we send them to?"

"Um, let me think about that for a second. Hm. Yeah, you know what? I know. You can send them to Rachel."

"YOU * PIG."**

That was Pete's actual girlfriend, Karen.

"YOU * PIG. HOW COULD YOU? IT IS OVER. I MEAN IT. OVER, PETE. OVER OVER OVER OVER OVER OVER OVER !@#$@#%!@#$."**

"What the f****?"

"Hi Pete, let me explain. My name is Kane, and we do a radio show where we catch cheaters in the act. Do you have anything to say for yourself?"

"Karen. Hey Karen. I can explain this. It's not what you think."

"OH REALLY. OH REALLY!"

It is at this point that I'm usually doubled over on the steering wheel laughing.

Because Pete will spend about ten minutes trying to tell Karen that she is crazy, he didn't do anything wrong. "Rachel" was just being "helpful," she "comforted" him in a time of need, yada yada, et cetera, and so on.

Intern John will say something like, "That dude was crazy. How did he ever think he would get away with that?"

For the audience it's a funny but useful reminder.

The truth is usually pretty simple.

When people have to complicate things to make them sound good, a personal agenda is at work.

We all know people with a lot of excuses, people who are windbags, people who make up every bullshit in the book.

Like my mother used to say,

"I'm sorry, I don't understand. Tell it to me like I'm

stupid."

It is easy to say this and to nod your head. In real life it gets a lot harder.

You deal with people who mystify the facts, who pump up the action and their role in the action, confuse meetings with results, add jargon where they could use plain English, name-drop and acronym-lay and generally wrap a Ph.D., MBA and JD all in one around information that should be straightforward and basic.

Whether it's your doctor, your lawyer, your kid's school or your own organization, you have to be willing to confront the possibility that the emperor is walking around totally naked.

What you do with that information – if you can find it, because you'll invariably be discouraged – is your business.

At the very least, have the courage to ask.

27

5 Productivity Secrets Your Boss Won't Tell You

When you're first starting out in your career, it's easy to think that your job consists of "what my boss tells me to do," followed closely by "how my boss tells me to do it." But after fifteen years of study, practice and mostly observation, I've concluded that the most productive employees in the world take a different tack. As follows:

1. Don't work for a boss you don't respect. It's true: There aren't an infinite number of jobs out there, and you don't always get to pick the boss you want. That said, you will inevitably fail at your job if you insist on working for someone you don't think very highly of. Because your feelings will inevitably leak out in your attitude, in your words, and in your work. And when your boss gets wind of the fact that you are contemptuous of them, nothing you do on the job will be right — even if all the work you do is brilliant. That situation alone is the ultimate productivity-killer.

2. Tell your boss what your boundaries are. All of us have tasks we need to decline. Sometimes they represent a higher volume of "ask" than we can shoulder. Other times, they're too outside our scope of work. Still other times, they violate our sense of integrity. If a request is not doable for you, it's important to say so explicitly.

3. Make a regular schedule for pursuing a passion outside the job. Engaged employees are productive employees, and it's a fact that no work environment can be endlessly engaging. You have something in your heart that you love to do, or maybe it's a few things, and it's nothing to do with work. Even if you feel like your tasks are overwhelming, and you're afraid you can't keep up, force yourself to do what you love for at least one hour a day. You will find that the energy, excitement and empowerment that comes from being fulfilled will "spill over" into the workplace. You'll bring more attention and accuracy to your work, because you'll have the confidence to take charge of the job — to do as well in the office as you do outside of it.

4. Learn the "iceberg" of your corporate culture. In organizational development we visualize the workplace as a kind of iceberg. Most of what you need to know is submerged beneath the surface, and you can be sure that nobody is fully capable of telling you what lies there. So while you should do the things you're explicitly told to do — that is, the tip of the iceberg — most of your time should be spent on the invisible levels. At a very broad level, these include the implicit requirements, meaning things you're supposed to know, and the unspoken ones, meaning things that cannot be articulated. The way

to explore these seemingly solidified and impenetrable masses is to ask about the implicit even if it makes you feel stupid. Once you understand that, you will be sophisticated enough to surmise the unspoken.

5. Organize your work into "projects" and "programs," and keep track of them. Everybody has things they need to do once and not again; these can be considered "projects" and their minutiae fill up most of your inbox with a flurry of emails back and forth. The rest of your work, and the more important part consists of "programs," that is things that you will repeat doing on a regular basis and that don't get as much attention. To be a productive employee you have to independently keep track of both of these things, and be able to report on them at a moment's notice. Every successful person I know has a binder or set of folders kept close to the desk, and they're ready to display the contents when the boss shows up and abruptly asks for a briefing.

While it's true that talent is something you're born with, the skills associated with being a great employee are most definitely learned. Anyone can become an invaluable asset, if they only take the time to study and practice.

28

On The Use of Memes In Government Communication

We begin with the assumption that government communication should be as good or better than private-sector communication, for three reasons:

- The public relies on the government as a trustworthy source of information
- Many are misinformed or under-informed about what the government does and the services it offers
- Trust in the government by the public is extraordinarily low

This is not only a bad situation, it is a dangerous one.

From that perspective, using the communication tools that are popular among ordinary citizens has the capacity to build trust. Whereas using highfalutin language – the equivalent of standing on a soapbox and preaching -builds mistrust.

Memes are a popular way to communicate in the age of social media. However, there are a couple of concerns that government rightfully has about them. This article aims to address them.

Issue #1: Copyright

A meme is a derivative work based on an original piece of art. At issue is whether the meme is a form of free speech, or an illegitimate commercialization of someone else's work.

To make a determination about whether the use is OK, the courts apply the doctrine of "fair use." They consider: "the purpose and character of the use (e.g., was it for profit?); the nature of the copyrighted work; the amount and substantiality of the portion of the work used in relationship to the whole work; and the effect of the use upon the potential market for or value of the copyrighted work." This is sometimes known as the "four-factor test."

The U.S. Copyright Office offers some examples of fair use, and an entry in Wikipedia sums them up: "Commentary, search engines, criticism, parody, news reporting, research, teaching, library archiving and scholarship." Let's look at how government memes stack up:

1. They are clearly for education, not profit
2. They are derivative works for the purpose of parody, to engage and educate the public. As the Copyright Office notes – "Copyright protects the particular way authors have expressed themselves. It does not extend to any ideas, systems, or factual information conveyed in a work."
3. Normally they represent a minimal use of the material, because they are single images.

4. Memes tend to boost the market for copyrighted work because they get traffic.

Issue #2: Good Taste

If copyright law is murky, the issue of taste is even murkier. Cutting-edge communication normally pushes the boundaries in order to get attention. Whether this boundary-pushing is desirable depends on at least the following three factors:

1. The urgency of the need to communicate – if there is a crisis of some kind
2. The feedback from the public – whether it's well-received
3. The cultural environment of the agency itself

What is OK in one agency or at one time may not be OK in another. The answer is always "it depends."

What Can You Do With Memes As A Government Communicator?

Here are some strategies for using memes. They're based on a review of the literature as well as informal discussion and collaboration. They are intended as a starting point for your own work, not as official advice or legal counsel:

1. Don't rely on "cat pictures" – develop an approach in which the visuals are substantively educational
2. Use memes sparingly – balance them with words that

inform

3. Humor is tricky, and can offend – use with caution
4. Make images that are very clear in their meaning – different people can have wildly different interpretations
5. Develop your own innocuous meme – a great case study is Home Depot's "Richard the Cat"

New things present new challenges and memes are definitely new. They are in many ways the essence of social media, subverting the "official voice" with one's reaction to it. They are a game-changer.

VI

Crisis

29

WikiLeaks and the Crisis of Government Communication

"Fewer than 3 in 10 Americans have expressed trust in the federal government in every major national poll conducted since July 2007—the longest period of low trust in government in more than 50 years." — Pew Research Center, Nov. 23, 2015

In the United States, federal government communicators have no shared professional standards of conduct, other than what they can piece together on their own.

This was one of the key findings of a groundbreaking study conducted by the Federal Communicators Network in 2016—the first-ever survey of federal communicators by federal communicators.

Out of 153 self-identified federal communicators who completed a small-scale survey administered by FCN:

- Just 1 percent—2 people—agreed "a great deal" with the assertion that "communication professionals' roles and expectations are generally consistent across government."

- They were more likely to strongly agree that individual performance expectations are clear (18 percent—27 people).
- But then again, there was overwhelming disagreement that those expectations are appropriate (11 percent—17 people).

(Click here to see the raw survey data in table format; look for question 5.)

If expectations are unclear it's because U.S. government information professionals utterly lack governmentwide standards and guidelines with which to do their jobs. This much became clear on diving into the confusing hodgepodge of research about what specifically it is that all federal information providers must do.

While superficially one may think that "accountability," "transparency," and "no spin" cover it—in fact there are times when the government is allowed to use appropriated funds to communicate in a way that can be (and often is) perceived as propagandistic or wasteful.

For example, the Smith Mundt Modernization Act of 2012 made it legal to distribute domestically U.S. government information intended for foreign audiences. While some decried the end of the "propaganda ban," others saw it as a reasonable modernization of the law, given that the Internet makes traditional information segregation impossible. (One could of course ask whether traditional government propaganda should cease altogether, since it is no longer covert.)

The U.S. government currently attempts to control for inappropriate communication using three distinct mechanisms:

- Accountability: The Federal Managers Financial Integrity Act of 1982 requires agencies to implement internal controls, including management communication, as a way of making sure that federal funds are spent properly.
- No Lobbying: The Anti-Lobbying Act of 1913, which was significantly updated in2002, prohibits the use of appropriated funds to try to persuade Congress to pass or not pass a particular law.
- No Propaganda: "Employment of Publicity Experts," Title 5 of the U.S. Code, Section 3107, originally dated 1913, states that "appropriated funds may not be used to pay a publicity expert unless specifically appropriated for that purpose." This language appears in federal appropriations bills annually.

Clearly this framework is not enough. Many have expressed concern about the extent to which taxpayer dollars are used inappropriately when it comes to federally sponsored communication:

"NASA tweeting that Congress should give it more money so our astronauts won't have to ride on Russian rockets. Recovery.gov reporting overly optimistic statistics on jobs saved and created by stimulus funds. The Department of Health and Human Service website encouraging the public to "state your support for health care reform" during the congressional debate over Obamacare. These are just some recent examples of the executive branch using our tax dollars to shape our opinions." — The Washington Post, *Sept. 24, 2015*

What happens when an agency goes too far? The Government Accountability Office launches an audit and issues a report, or Congress calls for research as agencies regularly do advertising, marketing and public relations. Right now the government is trying to figure out why exactly agencies spent $893 million on advertising contracts in fiscal year 2013 and almost $4.7 billion in total during the prior five fiscal years.

Research shows that 62 percent of the public has a positive view of federal employees. Considering that the public's view of the federal government is at a record low, it makes sense to establish a professional code of conduct and clear goals and objectives across the board for federal communicators. That would enable us to stand as gatekeepers when our agency is about to do something ill-advised. (These are my opinions only; I do not speak for my own agency or the government as a whole.)

In the U.K., such a code and a plan is already standard practice, and although the data are currently slim, one can reasonably assume there is a connection between communication and perceptions of integrity. For example, the Transparency International Corruption Perceptions Index 2015 ranks the U.S. beneath the U.K. when it comes to perceptions of integrity. While Britain is ranked among the top 10 performers in the world (tied for No. 10 with Germany and Luxembourg), the U.S. comes in lower (No. 16). This isn't by any means the worst performance on the chart (North Korea and Somalia are tied at No. 167), but the numbers do tell a story.

A fascinating dissertation by H.J.M. (Erna) Ruijer of Virginia Commonwealth University's Douglas Wilder School of Government and Public Affairs, offers some insight. It's called " Proactive Transparency and Government Communication in the USA and the Netherlands" (2013).

The author's research yielded some important findings. First, she showed that while the Netherlands is characterized by "principles-based" government communication (e.g. "do the right thing"), the U.S. is "rules-based" (e.g. "follow the letter of the law"). It is noteworthy that the Netherlands is ranked among the Top 10 in the Transparency Index as well.

In both countries, most communicators "valued proactive transparency highly and . . . were actively involved in implementing proactive transparency." Additionally, communicators "contributed to making information more findable, relevant and understandable for its users."

However, on the negative side, in both countries, "communicators indicated they sometimes leave out important details, give only part of the story or specifically highlight the positive elements in the information."

Perhaps most significantly, Ruijer found that a healthy organizational environment was necessary for communicators to deliver real information and avoid propaganda and spin. She writes:

> *"Communicators working in an organization that supports proactive transparency provide more substantial information, use less spin and are more inclined to solicit feedback and participation from stakeholders."*

The fact that the public does not trust the federal government, but instead awaits release after release of leaked information from Wikileaks, is a very real crisis for the U.S. government.

If you don't believe me—after all, the political communication associated with an election is completely separate from the information world of the civil service—I certainly hear the objection. Factually speaking, most of the interest Wikileaks stirs up is no doubt "political." Additionally, available data indicates that trust in individual agencies is high.

But I would still argue that all of us—both political appointees and those in civil service—are nevertheless considered by the public as part of that hard-to-pin-down-or-understand-brand known as "Washington, D.C." And sadly, the name of the city itself has developed a tainted connotation.

This crisis can, at least in part, be resolved by turning to federal communicators already on the payroll. We may not have an impact on perceptions of American politics, but we can make a difference in the world of the civil service. So equip us with the tools we need to ensure that federal government communication is reliable, and entrust us with the official role of gatekeeper.

Doing something is better than doing nothing. Improving federal communication is a step in the right direction. We all benefit from increased clarity, proactive transparency, accountability, and public trust.

Don't we?

30

7 Reasons Not To Blame "Rogue Employees" For Organizational Problems

When a word or phrase is used multiple times in the same way it starts to have the ring of messaging. And several times now, the word "rogue" has been used to blame federal government employees for wrongdoing carried out under the government's name:

Example #1, May 16, 2013:

- "News of (Acting IRS Director) Miller's resignation followed revelations that the IRS has identified two 'rogue' employees in the agency's Cincinnati office as being principally responsible for the 'overly aggressive' handling of requests by conservative groups for tax-exempt status, a congressional source told CNN". Miller in the same briefing stated that the employees were, quote unquote, "off the reservation." (CNN)

Example #2, August 27, 2012:

- "Since the controversy was first exposed, a divide has developed between the ATF staff in Phoenix who oversaw and implemented Fast and Furious; and their supervisors at ATF headquarters and the Justice Department. The Phoenix officials say higher-ups approved of the case. But the higher-ups say it was all the brainchild of rogue ATF officials in Phoenix." (CBS News)

Management writer Lawrence Serewicz points out that the term "rogue" is frequently used as an excuse for bad organizational behavior, i.e. "rogue ex-employee," "rogue trader," and so on. In "The Myth of the Rogue Employee: Rotten Barrels Create Rotten Apples," he explains why this is dangerous:

1. "All employees work and operate within an organisational context. For a rogue employee to exist, and operate, there has to be a lack of organisational (managerial) oversight."
2. "The 'rogue employee' is a dangerous myth because it is an attempt to cover systemic issues."
3. "When a rogue employee defence is used, it is also an admission that the internal communication system, where negative (or critical) information is not being communicated upwards, is not working."
4. "The rogue employee myth allows the fellow employees to feel that they have no responsibility for their colleagues' behaviour."
5. "It presents a false, deceptive, dangerous image to the

   public."

6. "The barrel becomes rotten before rotten apples emerge."

7. "The defence, undoubtedly developed for managerial reasons as well as legal reasons, (leaves) the organisation vulnerable to its unravelling. Once...proven otherwise, the whole defence crumbles."

At the end of the day, scapegoating people with this kind of language, even if technically accurate, creates more problems than it solves. Better to assume responsibility (quickly), make all information transparent, implement the necessary reforms, and move on.

31

5 Ways To Respond To The Critics: Lessons from McDonald's CEO

Superficially McDonald's and the government are different. But when you get closer they have at least one thing in common: an enormous, diverse customer base, many of whom rely on the institution for daily subsistence.

Normally the government is very cautious about responding to its critics. The reasons are infinite and familiar: many different interests at play – the need to speak in unison – the wild and provocative nature of some of the attacks – the impossibility of answering every one.

Plus there is this sense that to play defense is to lose. You don't want to get into mudslinging. (And add to that the fact that some back-and-forthing has to do with ongoing investigations, or confidential material that simply cannot be shared.)

All of this is why the speech by Don Johnson, CEO of McDonald's at the company's annual meeting was so refreshing. According to a report in Brandchannel.com, "Nutrition Critics Get No Apology From McDonald's CEO At Annual

Meeting," (May 24, 2013) Johnson aggressively took apart their comments point by point.

Here are some key takeaways perhaps applicable to other contexts:

1. **Validate Accurate Criticism:** A corporate responsibility group said McDonald's was promoting obesity. Johnson in effect validated that this used to be true.

2. **Show Improvement:** Johnson pointed out the healthier menu options now available to increase choice.

3. **Never Apologize For Your Mission:** The McDonald's also said clearly that the brand is about "fun," and that it's not a bad thing to let kids enjoy junky food every now and then. (Score one for simple rationality — it makes your critics look like ridiculous duds.)

4. **Point Out Attempts To Manipulate Your Story:** In response to charges that McDonald's directly aimed to exploit communities of color by marketing to them, Johnson said, point blank: "McDonald's is not the brand that you describe." Period.

5. **Establish a connection with your critics:** Johnson noted that he grew up in a low-income housing project in Chicago. The underlying message: I am one of you – I would not betray you. While this could backfire, it's effective if it's perceived as sincere – a way of breaching the gap between the corporate boardroom and its corporate accountability critics.

The bottom line is, large organizations should avoid excessive timidity about corporate messaging. It's OK to be "human" – nobody is perfect – and most people understand that at times "mistakes were made." While of course you can't defend wrongdoing, avoiding public remarks entirely is never a solution. Rather, admit it and go on.

The rest of the time, when the criticism involves a large area of gray, it is important to stand up for yourself. Talk about your efforts to improve, and never apologize for being who you are.

32

So Talking Points Are Evil Now?

I get a call the other day: "How are you?"

"Honestly," I say, slumping down in my Metro seat, "I am exhausted."

And I am exhausted. I'm so exhausted I can't remember what exhausted means. Everybody I know is exhausted. We seem to be running at a faster and faster pace and accomplishing just about...the same as before we were so exhausted.

...back to the conversation. The reply: "Well I can understand that, what with all the talking points going back and forth there in DC."

There I am, shoulders down. Literally waves of tiredness flowing upon me. It is late on a Friday, and the work is not done. Higher volume, limited resources, limited time. So much more to go.

What do I do all day? Make sure the facts are right...get the facts right.

We confuse the outcomes with the tools.

When a patient dies on the operating table, we don't stop doing surgery. We do ask – was the surgery necessary? Doctor qualified? Environment sanitary? Were there complications?

When a car goes over a cliff we do not stop driving either. (Actually I know someone who did stop driving when her car hit a side rail on the Beltway, swirled around and round in the rain, and got totaled. But that was temporary till she could work through all the trauma and the fear.) We do not outlaw cars.

And if a person is kidnapped from a grocery store parking lot, do we shut down all the grocery stores or stop shopping? Or maybe parking lots are bad?

So I ask this question now.

Why is it that every time there is a complex, sensitive issue or controversy, we veer away from the controversy itself and start questioning the need for standard communication tools?

Talking points are a critical piece of every communicator's knowledge base. Nobody should walk into a briefing without them.

Furthermore, if you're talking to the public in the early aftermath of a horrible and tragic incident, you will of course have to vet those talking points extensively – get everyone's input – and yes, of course you can have a dozen versions or more.

This post is not focused on any particular instance or incident. I'm not trying to secretly advocate a certain point of view. But I do want to call b.s. on the notion that professional communication is somehow suspect simply by the nature of its existence.

No matter what the polls say about trust in government – and it is at a historic low – we do take very seriously the content of our communication. What we say is carved in stone forever.

It's time we stop blaming surgery for malpractice, cars for car accidents, parking lots for kidnapping, and talking points for the content of the messaging.

VII

Diversity and Inclusion

<h1 style="text-align:center">33</h1>

Please Do Not Tell Me That You Are Colorblind

"Here in North Carolina's third-largest city, officers pulled over African-American drivers for traffic violations at a rate far out of proportion with their share of the local driving population. They used their discretion to search black drivers or their cars more than twice as often as white motorists — even though they found drugs and weapons significantly more often when the driver was white. Officers were more likely to stop black drivers for no discernible reason. And they were more likely to use force if the driver was black, even when they did not encounter physical resistance."
— *The Disproportionate Risks of Driving While Black*, The New York Times, *Oct. 25, 2015*

Racial discrimination is everywhere. So please don't tell me that you personally are "colorblind" or that the Black Lives

Matter movement is "racist."

According to the Bureau of Justice Statistics' most recent survey on public-police contact (2011), there is a disparity in perceptions by drivers about whether police are pulling them over for legitimate reasons or not. Only 68 percent of black drivers felt this way, versus 74 percent of Hispanic drivers and 84 percent of white drivers. And black drivers were three times as likely as whites to be searched: 6 percent versus 2 percent. (The search rate for Hispanic drivers was highest, at 7 percent.)

I once had the painful experience of listening to a colleague tell me about the "traffic-stop problem," which can reduce even the most dignified, accomplished human being to the equivalent of a cornered animal.

My colleague said that she routinely coached her son about how to dress. She was afraid that if he looked too casual (or wore any type of hoodie, obviously) he would get pulled over by the police and maybe shot.

She was afraid when he left home because she did not know if he would return.

We pride ourselves on overcoming racial discrimination in the workplace but the evidence shows we have far to go. Except when it comes to hiring, we tend to "pull over" white people as opposed to those who seem demonstrably black.

Remember "Are Emily and Greg more employable than Lakisha and Jamal?" (2003) This National Bureau of Economic Research paper tested whether "white-sounding" candidates would get more responses than "black-sounding" ones when applying for jobs.

Indeed, the candidates whose names were perceived to be white were 50 percent more likely to get called.

While this survey is dated, one of the study's primary researchers, Sendhil Mullainathan, told Politifact in 2015 that "large gaps" remain. Northwestern University professor David Figlio, also quoted in the article, said much the same thing.

So . . . racial discrimination: What can *you* do about it?

Two things:

First, please do not pretend that race, ethnicity, gender, and other categories of identity simply do not exist. That is not a plan. That is denial.

Second, please do not think you will ever understand the experience of another human being as they walk this planet.

Self-consciousness, real consciousness is what's needed. We can start by having a conversation with ourselves.

34

Abuse Survivors on the Job: Signs, Symptoms and How to Help

Maybe child abuse isn't such a problem. As of 2011, according to the Health and Human Services Department, there were 742,000 "confirmed cases of child maltreatment," which translates into about .1 percent of the child population.

Of course "there are lies, damned lies and statistics" and the numbers depend on both definition and methodology. For example, how would you define "maltreatment?" At a minimum, the categories are physical, emotional, sexual and neglect — but beyond that, the precise criteria vary from state to state.

And what is a "confirmed case?" According to the government, if you call social services and they issue a referral for assessment instead of doing a formal investigation, "it is often the case that no determination is made as to the allegations of maltreatment and therefore the child will not be classified as a victim."

Here are some statistics, gathered from governmental and nongovernmental studies by Childhelp.org, whose founders were recognized in 1983 by Health and Human Services for their "leadership in the prevention, treatment and research of child abuse and neglect, nationally and internationally."

Among the horrifying statistics cited by Childhelp — among them that "a report of child abuse is made every 10 seconds" — are the results of one large-scale study carried out from 1995 to 1997 by the Centers for Disease Control and Prevention jointly with Kaiser Permanente.

For this study, 17,000 patients self-reported childhood abuse during the course of a doctor's physical. Even taking into account the fact that these allegations are not necessarily proved in a court of law, as well as the fact that the study was conducted nearly 20 years ago, the disparity between the numbers generated by official investigations and victims' own accounts is shocking.

According to them, here's what our nation's children may actually be experiencing:

- More than 1 in 4 children physically abused (28.3%)
- More than 1 in 5 children sexually abused (20.7%)
- More than 1 in 10 emotionally neglected (14.8%) or abused (10.6%)
- Nearly 1 in 10 physically neglected (9.9%)

Let's assume that the workplace population is generally reflective of these percentages, and let's also assume that most people work in a team setting. The generally accepted norm for immediate team size is five people, but most of us interact with a slightly larger group of colleagues from other teams in order to get things done.

So it is likely that at least one person you work with on a

somewhat regular basis has been abused as a child. The long-term symptoms of such trauma do not just "go away," and the victims cannot just "get over it."

Bracha Goetz explains why: "Traumatic experiences remain encoded in a primitive part of our brain, the amygdala, which automatically goes into "fight or flight" mode when triggered by certain stimuli, even decades later ... The lower part of our brainstem, unlike our far more complex prefrontal cortex, doesn't have the level of sophistication needed to be able to tell the difference between triggers that signal real danger and those that do not. Footsteps above, or even a particular place or food, can elicit an automatic response that floods the body with terror, since those stimuli are neurologically linked to the approach of the abuser."

As adults, she notes, survivors experience a range of unwanted symptoms including "depression, PTSD, dissociative disorders, eating disorders, drug addictions and anxiety."

For adults who have been sexually abused as children, write Melissa and Joshua Hall, the impact includes not only depression, but also a range of symptoms that affect survivors' relationships with others. Among them: "guilt, shame, self-blame ... anxiety, repression, denial."

Of course, survivors of childhood abuse do not normally walk around with a tattoo that says "I was victimized." In fact, the shame they feel — as well as the ongoing social and workplace stigmas surrounding any discussion of one's personal traumatic experiences — virtually guarantees that they will go to great lengths to appear "normal" at work.

So you will probably not know. But you may very well see evidence of post-traumatic stress disorder in a colleague. Amy Menna and others at Gift From Within outline some of these in an article titled "Post Traumatic Stress Disorder and the Workplace: What Employers and Coworkers Need to Know":

- **Information retention:** Memory problems, difficulty retaining information, lack of concentration.
- **Emotional responses:** Feelings of fear or anxiety, panic attacks, unreasonable reactions to situations that trigger memories.
- **Physical issues:** Physical problems, trouble staying awake.
- **Relationship issues:** Poor interactions with co-workers
- **Disruption to the workplace:** Absenteeism, interruptions if employee is still in an abusive relationship, harassing phone calls, etc.

Of course, it is neither sensitive nor advisable to directly confront a co-worker or employee with the concern that they may have been abused — even in the name of helping them. But if you think you are working with a potential victim, the authors of "PTSD and the Workplace" have some advice:

1. **Invest in training.** Given that one in four employees has potentially been abused in some way and given that abuse affects the ability of an individual to function in all aspects of life, this seems like a sensible move regardless of whether a certain person seems to be

exhibiting symptoms. (I would add that supervisory training and co-worker training will likely need to differ due to HR considerations — for example you don't want an employee to get the opposite impression from what you intend (e.g., that they've somehow been targeted.)

2. **If an employee tells you that they need practical help, listen to them.** They offer the example of an assault victim who doesn't want to work nighttime hours, or who asks to be walked to her car (or the bus stop).

3. **Be aware of what symptoms look like, and be prepared to accommodate them.** The authors give the example of providing an office environment that has less distractions, or more time to finish a task.

4. **Ask what you can do to help the employee do their best work.** The authors point out that survivors will feel embarrassed to admit they need help at all, so it is important to keep asking, but not in a way that seems overly persistent and aggressive. A good training program will help supervisors and co-workers alike to find the right balance.

5. **Address problems immediately.** The authors point out a commonly known best practice, to provide "gentle and immediate feedback" if and when performance isn't up to par or the employee seems to be having a hard time. They may never talk about PTSD at all, but the open dialogue and your sensitivity to various potential causes of problems are both beneficial to helping the employee as well as helping restore the office to a more productive state.

The bottom line is this: All of us walk through life with

baggage — physical and emotional —no exceptions. Like my father-in-law, may he rest in peace, used to say: "The chances are a million to one, but there are a million and one things."

So it's wise to have compassion for others, if for no other reason than karma.

But if you're looking for a business justification for sensitivity to co-workers who have survived (or are going through) some form of abuse, think about this: Just like with diversity, treating others with care and compassion is ultimately good for business. It's smart management:

- At the very least, it reduces disengagement and time lost due to stress and the resultant physical symptoms, not to mention the impact on health insurance rates.
- At best, it promotes worker trust, loyalty, team performance and the retention of institutional knowledge that can benefit both long-term strategy and the immediate successful implementation of complex projects requiring detailed knowledge of company history, culture and operations.

At the end of the day, caring about others at work does not mean you look away and let them get away with poor job performance. It does mean you pay attention to what is going on, with their behavior and their work, and take positive and reasonable steps to support their productivity.

35

Is Religion Unsafe for Work?

Last week I had to get my mind off the San Bernardino shootings, and so I forced myself to watch a Vince Vaughn comedy on Xfinity called *Unfinished Business.*

I wasn't especially familiar with this film but as a brand Vince Vaughn is a certain kind of funny and I was sure that the time would produce the intended effect. It did.

In the movie he and his sidekicks need to sign a client or go bankrupt. Nothing can go wrong with this deal.

On the plane to Portland, where the deal is to be done, Vaughn turns to his sales director.

"Listen, Mike, when we get to the meeting, don't say your last name."

"What's wrong with my last name?"

"It's distracting from business," says Vaughn.

"What's distracting about my name?" says the guy.

"Your name is Mike Pancake."

I saw this scene and couldn't help but laugh hysterically. It's funny on the plane and it's funny when of course the guy screws up and says "Mike Pancake." (And they don't get that desperately needed handshake, either — at least not yet.)

But what isn't funny about the bit is the subtle message "diverse" people get in real life: We want you, we welcome you, but please don't bring your "difference" to the workplace.

I remember my uncle worked for the U.S. government in the Senior Executive Service. An Orthodox Jew, he would not wear a yarmulke for fear of provoking anti-Semitism.

When I joined the U.S. government I covered my hair in a religious way that was unusual for America (an Israeli type snood). One woman asked me, "Excuse me, I don't mean to offend you — but are you a Mennonite?"

My father's side of the family is Chasidish (Hasidic). I have never once seen a Chasid in the government. If I did, they were hiding it very well.

I have worked a few times with very religious Christians. One woman started a prayer group at work — they gave her a quiet room once a week on Wednesdays. But only after her boss almost nixed the whole thing.

And I have worked with Muslims as well. They are in a terrible situation, worse now than ever — pressured from all sides into an impossible vise. Walking on landmines, constantly.

You have to let people be themselves at work. You have to let them live their faith, if they have it. It's not just about obeying the law, where applicable; or doing better at business, because you will; or even because you're nice enough to "tolerate" others being "other."

It's right to support diversity, in the workplace and everywhere, because diversity is fundamentally human. If we turn against each other because of religious garb, we will turn against each other for every other reason under the sun, and then where will the turning end?

It is OK to live and let live — not everybody has to be the same, like Wonder Bread.

People say that terrorists want to force religion on others. But I think it's the opposite: The freedom to live your conscience is precisely what they want to steal.

When we uphold religious diversity at work — including the absence of religion completely — we stop them.

36

Branding to Recruit Across the Generations

Many argue that the presenting problem is a talent gap, i.e. the Boomers are going to retire, soon. There won't be Millennials waiting to replace them, because they've lost patience with the system. Presumably the civil service will fall apart absent a solid talent pipeline to back up the Gen Xers who will need to take over when the Boomers retire.

I disagree, even though parts of the problem are presented in a way that I agree with (e.g. the part about Millennials not having patience for the system.)

- For one thing, Boomers frequently want or need to work beyond retirement age, sometimes well beyond. So I am not convinced they're leaving as quickly as people may think.
- For another, some aspects of the system work well for Millennials, who are highly team-oriented, and prefer clear-cut criteria and expectations – defining characteristics of the civil service.

The real issue, I think, is that a variety of external forces are combining to change the nature of work rapidly and permanently. These changes cut across all generations. And the federal civil service has trouble understanding or keeping up with them.

An article in Fast Company sums them up well. Briefly:

1. Work is more remote than on-site.
2. Employees are expected to be on-call 24/7.
3. Work is expected to be "a calling" not just what you do from 9 to 5.
4. Work/life boundaries are increasingly nonexistent as friendship is being replaced by "networking."
5. Work is increasingly project-to-project (i.e. temporary) rather than long-term or even permanent.

Related trends:

1. Nomadic living – you set up shop in a remote area and telecommute
2. Communal working/workspaces – you find other free-lancers and co-rent space with them
3. Full-time job + side work – you have a hobby or two that you do for money, while keeping a steady income flowing (yes, this is supposed to be your passion, ideally…I suppose)

In the federal civil service, a related major issue is the relation-ship between contractors and federal employees – because work culture is not manual – in order for it to be productive there has to be seamless collaboration – one team, one culture, one mission.

Given all of this, in my mind, the real question is how we define civil service as distinct from non-civil service. If it is fair to say that a key distinction is the desire for an "inherently governmental cadre of dedicated employees" then a more robust model might be a federal-wide approach, where we recruit people into the civil service in an agency-agnostic way, and then deploy them across agencies in a manner that builds a core set of skills as appropriate.

Looked at in this way, you hire for dedication and you train for skills, and you start people right out of high school. Because you want a permanent workforce with institutional knowledge that is specific to government, not a disposable one that can pretty much work anywhere.

Which would make Pathways incredibly important.

As well as employee assistance program type programming.

...a lot of other implications.

But it goes well beyond retaining Millennials.

Once you define the structural problem and then the desired solution you're ready to start defining that solution in terms of brand.

37

Can Gen X Succeed at Work?

There are three main generations in the workforce today:

- The "overstudied" baby boomers (born 1946-1964)
- Overly "coddled" millennials (born 1981-1997)
- The nearly totally ignored Gen Xers (born 1965-1980)

I am a Gen Xer. And the fact that I am ignored by the media has been covered many times, including this *TIME* cover story in 1997.

This is not to bemoan such a sad state of affairs. Nor is it to enlighten you about all things X. And, of course, one would be stupid to reduce people to simplistic generational categories.

Rather, it is to highlight a problem Gen Xers face with respect to workplace diversity, precisely because we are so little-studied and understood: our communication style. Compared with "political" baby boomers and "polite" millennials, Gen Xers are perceived as "rude," "skeptical," "cynical."

Most of the time, discussions of generational difference do not focus on language. Here is typical depiction (emphasis on boomers, Xers and millennials is mine).

But it is important to talk about differences in communication style, because as we all know, the impact of miscommunication on workplace productivity is significant. Not the least of the potential problems is that employees can make costly and dangerous mistakes.

The impact of miscommunication on an individual's career may be invisible, but it is personal and it is costly. Which is probably why *Harvard Business Review* has an entire section on its website specifically devoted to this.

Unfortunately for the Gen Xer, particularly the Xer who is working in a team-based organization, conversations about diversity in communication style tend to revolve around cross-cultural issues or those relating to gender.

Given that the unique constellation of Gen X characteristics tends to be ignored in the diversity conversation, and given that Xers' unique style of communication is essentially a nonissue, it follows that this generational cohort is bound to suffer from being "branded" negatively in some very unfair ways.

The solution to this problem does not lie in "consciousness raising," from my point of view. It isn't a matter of one group trying to oppress another. Rather, it's about taking personal responsibility for understanding that our colleagues may have trouble understanding why we talk the way we do.

It's about recognizing that no matter how many achievements you can list on your résumé, your communication style may actually tick people off. And that you sometimes have to temper yourself to get along with them.

38

The Normative Fallacy That Gets In The Way Of Diversity Programming

The hidden premise of diversity programs is an imaginary figure (the normative figure) who sets the standard.

This is never articulated outright. And we don't even like to admit it to ourselves.

But it is there, and it's why messages around equal employment opportunity are often so out-of-touch and stale.

In the protective sense, i.e. in the interest of ensuring the employee is not prevented from enjoying equal opportunity, diversity messaging should emphasize that:

- Nobody is the "norm" — we are ALL diverse, even if you can't see it on the outside
- There are endless categories of diversity — way beyond the protected groups in the EEO statutes
- Within categories, there is substantial variation — e.g. the Jewish community is relatively tiny, but incredibly diverse

In the productivity sense, i.e. in the interest of enlightening the organization, diversity messaging should emphasize that organizations too often leave money lying on the floor because they don't know how to leverage diversity well.

Here's a great and very simple example. Childbirth and the raising of children, rather than being treated as a "time-out" or "other activity" could be integrated into the workplace with:

- Private wellness rooms not only for lactation, but also for a quiet time-out
- On-site childcare, open to any caregiver of a child
- Community area in the cafeteria so parents can spend time with kids during the work day
- Work/life support group for caregivers
- After-hours care line for referrals to support providers of working parents

To fully do this means to get away from the false dichotomy between "us" and "them," the "regular person" and the "different one," the "able-bodied" and those for whom "accommodations are made."

Long way of saying, in a truly diverse workplace, all of us are "freaks and geeks" — and none of us are.

VIII

Future

39

Inventing The Networked, Streamlined Federal Enterprise—a.k.a., "Government 3.0"

The federal government has long made use of vendors to provide everything from equipment to IT support. Today, it is expanding on that reliance and increasingly moving toward a futuristic business model that emphasizes interagency cooperation, shared services, and even shared workspaces:

- Agencies paying other agencies to do work for them, such as standing up websites or shooting video.
- Agencies pooling resources to stand up programs that touch on multiple missions.
- Departments consolidating support functions such as acquisitions and HR.
- Vendors being tasked with a wide range of not only service assignments—such as IT and communications—but also leadership assignments, such as change management.
- Open-air, modular workspaces that encourage collab-

oration and discourage territorial "ownership" by any employee of a single office.

Where did all of this change come from? After all most people still think of government as a lumbering, stove-piped bureaucracy, ill-equipped to meet citizens' demands. With the advent of the Internet, that is rapidly changing:

- The first era of government was offline and decentralized. Let's call it Government 1.0.
- The second era of government was internet-enabled but uncoordinated. Government 2.0.
- The new era of government is networked, streamlined, nimble and rapidly responsive. Let's call it Enterprise Government, or Government 3.0.

While this trend might be a good thing — it certainly sounds like a good thing in some respects — it is clearly also saddled with risk:

- **Technically Capable But Substantively Unqualified Staff:** Permanent loss of employees who have a deep and nuanced understanding of the agency's history, mission and goals — leading to employees at all levels who may be technically qualified but lack the ability to make informed decisions.
- **A Culture of Expediency:** Sacrifice of agency's long-term goals to quick, convenient decision-making.
- **Push-A-Button Management:** Rather than build a skilled cadre of team members who are engaged, motivated and able to handle mission needs, we "bring

in the robots" who simply do whatever we tell them, without asking why. There is nobody to challenge bad decisions.

- **Fiefdoms:** Consolidation of services means lack of competition for those services, and accordingly the repression of employees who will lack mobility from place to place. For example, if all human capital functions are consolidated into one service office, and there is an abusive supervisor at large, it will be impossible to move out of that office without leaving the government.

- **Overspending:** The substitute workforce charges a premium for its work, and the customer agency, preferring expediency and lacking knowledge of how much money a service should cost, accedes readily. The taxpayer is shortchanged.

- **Lack of Transparency:** Where is the money going? Who was responsible for making that decision? Did so much have to be spent? Who owns the open data? When the answer can be provided by opening up an agency budget, it's easier to be transparent. But when responsibility for the books starts to be shared, things get more complicated. Not impossibly so—given that nowadays everything is stored somewhere on a computer—but potentially challenging.

- **The End Of "Inherently Governmental":** As more and more tasks are taken on by outside parties, and seemingly done capably, there is a tendency to simply increase both the number and kinds of tasks. There is no internal negotiation, no scuffling: the contractor handles it. But the entire purpose of having "inherently governmental" work protected is to ensure that the government serves the interest of the people.

Fueled by the adrenaline rush of technology, it is possible that we are throwing out the baby with the bathwater. Despite this, Enterprise 3.0 is likely only going to accelerate. For these reasons:

- **Optics:** People like it when the government seems to be cutting costs. Consolidation and shared services looks good, especially since the government has a reputation for waste.
- **Technology:** With a "save money" metric in hand, Big Data tells us exactly where funds can be redirected more efficiently to get things done. At an enterprise level, that means funding multi-agency initiatives or shared services desks rather than piecemeal programs.
- **Speed:** Within a typical agency, the pressure is normally towards inertia, because change is experienced as inherently negative. This is why staff-initiated projects often die on the vine. Outsourcing, shared efforts, and cooperative initiatives move the change factor outside the agency, creating less risk of internal derailment.

There are five things that need to happen in order for Government 3.0 to work:

- **Transparency:** It has to be very clear where money is being spent, and why. This can be accomplished through public online dashboards.
- **Accountability:** Establishing clear roles and responsibilities is essential to avoid vague utterances and finger-

pointing in case decisions go bad.

- **Empowerment:** In an environment of rapid and unpredictable change, employee feedback is needed more than ever to keep the ship on a steady course. That means reversing the top-down leadership model and replacing it with small, matrixed organizations where every person has a say.

- **Return of the Civil Service**: Having a modular government can actually be quite freeing for the employee who may have otherwise been stuck in a certain job for years at a time without moving.

- **Leadership:** Senior executives draw a big salary, and therefore have a lot to lose. Not only that, but if they are let go, the stigma attached is huge. Money plus potential loss of status are a major deterrent to leaders taking the kind of bold actions necessary to transform the government workplace. A better way to handle leadership would be for all senior executives to occupy such spots for a temporary period, then be reassigned to the ranks. This would also create mobility for professionals who have senior leadership potential—and who, given the proper training and experience, might surprise us with what they can achieve.

IX

National Security

40

Why We're Losing the Brand War Against ISIS

The supreme art of war is to subdue the enemy without fighting."
— *Sun Tzu, The Art of War (513 BC)*

Defeating ISIS messaging should be a piece of cake — right? After all, everybody says "they're a bunch of loony radicals." How hard can it be to unmask them for what they are?

But we are struggling. As *The Washington Post* reported (Dec. 2, 2015), a panel of private sector branding experts commissioned by the State Department to review anti-ISIS messaging did not come back with a positive report.

According to one official quoted on background, the group "had serious questions about whether the U.S. government should be involved in overt messaging at all."

While the State Department has declined to release the actual report, *The New York Times* (June 12, 2015) reported receiving a "sensitive but unclassified" memo dated three days earlier from a source in the Obama administration. In it, Richard Stengel, undersecretary of State for Public Diplomacy and Public Affairs, says bluntly: "The coalition [to fight ISIS through coordinated messaging] does not communicate well internally or externally."

From an external communication perspective, says Stengel, "our narrative is being trumped by ISIL's. We are reactive — we think about 'counter-narratives,' not 'our narrative.' "

But it is worse than that. In a Gizmodo commentary on the *Post* story, Kate Knibbs tore into the government's failed attempts to respond to ISIS messaging effectively:

> *"Scrolling through the questions and answers [on Ask.fm, an anonymous Q&A website used by the State Department as one way of combating ISIS through social media] is an exercise in rapidly losing confidence in the governments' ability to wage a propaganda war."*

Here is an example of one well-intentioned but nevertheless groan-worthy interchange:

There's no other way to put it: Surely we mean well, but the government is just so very uncool — so incredibly out of touch — when it comes to doing what it takes to fight ISIS and win.

The first mistake we made was underestimating them. ISIS recruitment tactics, targeted both at young men and women, are working; they are experiencing "frighteningly rapid global growth," despite President Obama famously calling them the "JV [junior varsity] team."

Their recruitment tactics are highly sophisticated, speaking the language of their targets, using the preferred communication methods of their audiences, telling them precisely what they want to hear. Boys are lured by the promise of sex; girls, ironically, are told that joining the group is akin to feminism.

Just like any strong brand narrative, ISIS content represents messages that matter to the target, and that are extremely different from what they hear, at least in the Western mainstream. It isn't just one thing, of course — there are dimensions of empowerment, of religion, of making the world a more just and less decadent place.

ISIS also is the classic cult: offering a self-contained, secret world, initially appealing but with no chance of escape, to a population that frequently feels lost, alienated, and perpetually in transition. In a world where the choices can feel like a blizzard of dead ends, ISIS inserts itself as a ready-to-wear community with a winning path toward the future.

They do not operate arbitrarily or off-the-cuff, either: ISIS has more than one playbook, each for specific ends, and they follow the strategy carefully.

We've made a lot of other mistakes as well, some of which *The Washington Post* covers pretty comprehensively, especially here and here.

They include:

- **Denying reality:** underestimating the enemy, refusing to not only name the enemy but describe the nature of its identity, failing to talk about our role in creating the problem, overestimating our successes, delaying for a lengthy period of time to admit that we are at war.
- **Playing defense:** failing to tell our story, over-focusing

on the enemy's tools of choice, insisting on explaining over and over again "why they're wrong and we are right."

- **Incompetence:** "talking the brand talk" but failing to put expert communicators in charge; confusing the message with the medium; unrealistic ideas about metrics; overemphasizing logic versus emotion, or emphasizing the wrong emotional points; condescending to the audience.
- **Bureaucracy:** Letting infighting derail the process, overemphasizing internal reactions, short-term thinking, delaying the formation of the team for a significant period of time, failing for too long to insist on staff and money from partners, failing to effectively leverage the national and international partners on the team.
- **Insularity:** Refusing to bring in competent help from the outside for too long, failing to give the private sector the reins and invest in their expertise as needed.

ISIS is a new kind of enemy, and it was inevitable that we would make mistakes in fighting them — yes, even significant ones. We can't afford to look back and indulge in hand-wringing. It's time to chart a new course.

We begin at the beginning: In branding, as in war, constantly playing defense is a good way to get killed. This is because brand equity depends on constantly telling the consumer why they should pick you — not on telling them why they shouldn't pick your competitors.

By communicating proactively and positively with the customer, you develop the three key characteristics of a strong brand. This is the framework provided by top market research firm Millward Brown:

- **Salient:** It's top-of-mind when it's time to buy.
- **Meaningful:** It's the most meaningful to you — you're emotionally and intellectually attached to it.
- **Different:** It's the one that stands out as unique.

Al Ries, one of the world's preeminent authorities on branding, explained the importance of playing offense in *Positioning: The Battle for Your Mind.* Not only that, said Ries, but the key to success is knowing your customers, knowing how they think, and shaping their perceptions. As he put it: "Positioning is not what you do to a product. It's what you do to the mind of your prospect."

With that in mind, here is what we need to do right now:

- **Be honest:** The enemy is not just a particular group. It is a brand that can loosely be described as "radical Islam." Elements of this group are fundamental to Islam itself, albeit the nonviolent version. We must understand who we are dealing with and shut them down.
- **Playing offense:** There is a version of Islam that does not embrace elements that pose a threat. Many Muslims live their lives by this version. We need to immerse ourselves in their story, and combine it with the story of America, integrating the two in such a way that our nation evolves. What began as a "Christian nation" can no longer be described that way: We are a patchwork of religions and cultures and the story of that diversity is more compelling than an ideology of hate.

- **Competence:** The government must hire, from within, professional communicators well-versed in branding — not just antiterrorism experts or Middle East subject matter experts. You shouldn't drive a car unless you have a driver's license.
- **Prioritize Efficiency and Effectiveness:** Those of us who work in government are familiar with the ways bureaucracy thwarts success. The administration must act to eliminate the barriers faced by the State Department in its public diplomacy mission.
- **Controlled Openness:** There is a balance to be struck here between the one extreme of insularity, and the other extreme of letting the private sector "take over." The balance is achieved by having a government communicator oversee a large and diverse team, with a clear chain of command and well-defined roles and responsibilities.

In his address to the nation on Dec. 6, President Obama assured us that we would ultimately defeat ISIS. Reassurances are nice, and I believe the news reports suggesting that the president is frustrated by our messaging failures thus far. But as they say, "the definition of insanity is doing the same thing over and over again and expecting a different result."

We can do a better job at this. We can render ISIS irrelevant. But if we're going to do it, we need to go in strong, play hard and finish the job.

Stengel is correct: The task is not about crafting a good "counter-narrative."

It is about giving the microphone to Muslims all over the world who seek to redefine Islam itself in the eyes of the world. In a sense, what's needed here is to rebrand a religion and our nation at the same time: Islam as peaceful, in the manner suggested by many prominent religious reformers, and the United States as inclusive and respectful of many faiths.

We ought to invest in this. Branding is much more important to our security than fighting: It can save many lives, and leave us with a lasting peace.

Telling a better story isn't just about selling soap flakes. It can be about changing the world for the better. And when we embrace a better narrative — all of us, not just the USA — we will see an end to terrorism once and for all.

X

Internal Communication

41

Communicating to a Cynical Workforce

We don't need to debate this, do we? Many people are checked out at work. They don't take the time to read your carefully crafted messages very carefully, if they read them at all. They can barely be bothered to take the all-employee survey with its detailed questions and responses.

And if you tell me that employees work for their managers, not the company, and they mostly want to hear from the boss who's giving them a performance evaluation at the end of the year, point taken. But are employees really engaged with the information they receive from their managers? Maybe the information is timely and relevant to their jobs, but does it have that higher ring of truth and meaning?

Consider the fact that at any given moment a substantial percentage of employees are angry. They don't like the way they're being treated, or they don't feel valued on the job, or someone at work is harassing them, maybe even the boss. Perhaps they are underpaid or their job title is inappropriate for the work they do. They are probably keeping their eyes open for another, better job; or maybe they're actively looking.

If they've been in the organization for any length of time, they've seen senior leaders come and go and with these executives the grand initiatives that were supposed to fix everything.

It is hard to imagine what kind of internal communication could break through the clutter, the spoil and the noise and truly get people to open up and work together.

Some might say that the answer is radical honesty, or openness or some version of transparency combined with emotional intelligence. But that answer leaves the broken system largely intact.

The way to communicate effectively with cynical employees is, first, for the people who run the organization to secure, in writing, a commitment to justice—starting now.

Justice means that unethical employees are eliminated from the system. This includes the bullies, the cheats, the liars, the incompetent and those who simply refuse to do their fair share. All of them are bound to new rules of behavior, and those rules are written to benefit customers and employees alike, without doing anything to hurt the surrounding community or environment.

The proclamation of justice should be posted in a public place, and the organizational changes should then commence immediately, carried out by a governance board comprised of employee representatives of all types and levels.

Depending on the type of organization one is dealing with, the specifics of this will differ.

After the detritus of the organization has been removed, decisions must be made concerning fair and appropriate compensation. Again, how this is done will necessarily vary. I am not an economist, an accountant or a budgeting officer. But most people can understand that the greater the risk, the greater the reward and that nobody's labor should be exploited.

So now we are left with a pool of reasonable people, ready and willing and able to work, comfortable with the compensation scheme.

At this point, decisions must be made about business strategy, and how it is going to change to conform to the new (i.e. just and fair and open) environment. How will the organization return value to its stakeholders?

Again, this is where representatives of the employee community come in, to think through the key issues and return with sensible decisions. Somebody has to be in charge of reviewing them and making the final call; most people understand that a certain amount of authority in the organization is inevitable and necessary.

Throughout this entire process, and the unfolding drama of events that is the day-to-day life of the organization, communication has to flow freely. If it doesn't and people are hiding things or holding information to themselves to gain an advantage, the organization itself stands to fail.

Here's the bottom line: Internal communication is not the equivalent of icing on the cake. Rather it is the main course of the dinner. It has to be connected to the fundamental decisions that are made every single day about how the organization will function. It has to be connected to a set of values to which all adhere, or are shown the door. It has to be inextricably linked to a sense of justice, the belief that all are accountable for the things they do and that accountability is not just the basis for membership in the organization but fundamental to its business model.

If you're still somehow thinking that you can ignore this kind of reality, the result will be a continuation of the same-old, same-old status quo. Checked-out, complaining, complacent employees who are happy to take a paycheck, but not so happy to show up at work and do their jobs. Talented individuals who have a lot of qualifications to contribute to your enterprise, but who have decided not to buy in to anything you say, because they know you aren't really invested in them.

42

7 Values Transforming Today's Workplace

Radical transparency" is one of those really good ideas that few organizations actually implement because it consists of taking drastic steps to promote the availability of internal data. It is wildly exciting to the public, but in my experience, most executives just don't get why they should knock down the doors to explain their screw-ups.

Put aside their legitimate fears: demotion, firing, litigation, unpleasant publicity. Part of the problem with getting organizations to open up is that they genuinely don't understand the values that underpin our expectations. For example, despite the fact that the deed is already done, I do believe that the public would appreciate knowing how exactly $6.5 trillion dropped out of view at the Pentagon.

Consider also the low uptake of "holacracy," the currrent trend toward destroying the management hierarchy to promote empowered self-management by teams. In 2015, according to a Gallup survey, only 32 percent of U.S. employees were actually engaged in their work. There is no way to say this nicely: Disengaged employees don't care. But they are taking a salary from the company just the same.

Again, I do believe that the gap in results that we are seeing has to do with a lack of understanding of the values that underpin employees' expectations of the workplace. We have moved on from the factory-based economy. Service, knowledge and collaboration workers expect and need to exercise some measure of control over their efforts, including the space they work in. Yet oddly, the dominant values of most organizations continue to be authoritarian, hierarchical and even arbitrary — like Starbucks' micromanagey employee dress code.

There are multiple value shifts associated with stakeholders' new expectations of organizations.

Here is a brief explanation of each shift:

Empowerment versus authority: The individual and the small team make decisions rather than having decisions dictated to them from on high.

Disclosure versus concealment: Telling what's going on, the earlier the better, leads to forgiveness whereas hiding the truth is unforgivable. The cover-up is worse than the crime.

Frailty versus bluster: People are respected for admitting their faults, and projects are similarly honored as bold attempts even if they do not fully succeed. Those who brag, but have little or nothing to show for it, are quickly outed and mocked.

Insight versus information: The numbers themselves no longer tell the story. People who understand the numbers and can offer useful insight based on studying them in context are prized.

Truth versus loyalty: The public today simply wants to

know the truth. Whereas in the past, keeping secrets out of loyalty to the organization was a mark of pride (you would "throw somebody under the bus" so that they could "take one for the team"). Today, this would be considered disgusting.

Advancing a cause versus promoting yourself: In the recent past, it was fashionable to use work as a platform for Brand Me. Today, employees and customers alike expect organizations to be giving something back. Meaning is a primary value; selfishness is not.

Sharing versus hoarding: The notion of a sharing economy extends to workplace spaces, assignments, and distribution of wealth associated with project success. Put simply, people expect to co-work and receive a share of the profits, and they enjoy being part of this kibbutz-like collaborative effort. On the other hand, holding all the money back for oneself, or all the credit, or all the power, is loathsome, and people will take great pains to distance themselves from such a person.

As the above is only the product of my own observation and amalgamation of the content I see crossing over the transom, more study is clearly needed. Hopefully these thoughts will spark further research and discussion.

43

Your Subordinates Know More About You Than You Know

I know you only by the way you treat me, nothing else.

I'm not listening to most of what you say.

You asked me to find the core values brochure. It's in the closet, buried under pens and colored folders and paper clips.

Here's how I know what you care about (yes *you*, a representative of leadership): How. You. Act.

You don't know what I mean? You think you never see me? I know you by:

- The things other people say about you. Your reputation.
- The way you choose to greet people in the hallway.
- The way you talk about other people.
- The way you listen—or don't.
- What you do in response to problems.
- The way you show empathy to those in pain.
- Your attitude to new ideas that are not yours.
- The way you enforce the rules.
- Whether you study a matter carefully, or are impulsive

and just act out.
· Who you give the microphone to, and where you shine your spotlight.

Yes, I know you. Every single day, I watch your values unfold. And I am learning.

44

Stop Pretending Your Colleagues Are Your Family

It's a funny thing at this agency," she said. "You've got to be reaaaallllly careful who you talk to. Those people you see every day at work, they have friends you don't see. You catch my drift?"

"No." I felt completely stupid. Was she talking about the Mafia?

My friend shook her head. "Let me spell it out. These people have all worked here for a lot of years. And a lot of years is a very long time. Let's just say that many of them are close."

"I just cannot believe it," I said. "These people seem so..."

"So what? So boring?"

"Well, yeah, kinda." I looked over at another table, at a man attacking some orange chicken with his tie thrown over his suit. There was a folded-up newspaper on the table, which he appeared to be reading as he shoveled.

"Him? No."

"Remember these words forever," said my friend, grabbing my wrist a bit too firmly. "Because I am about to retire, and nobody else will tell it to you like it is. You never know who's sleeping with who in this town. So never burn your bridges, and never assume you know jack shit about anything."

***

I wish I could say that I'd made that story up, or that my "friend" was only a single person. But the truth is I've heard the same type of thing over and over again, and it hasn't mattered where I worked, in the public or the private sector.

Surveys bear this out: Though most couples are first introduced by friends, some meet in the workplace as well.

Of course, there are close relationships at work that have nothing whatsoever to do with sex. Many people have simply worked together for many years, and have a comfort level with one another. Perhaps they're even "office spouses."

Certainly we frequently see movie depictions of coworkers who socialize outside the office too. In fact, nowadays it's almost impossible to watch a movie without seeing colleagues portrayed in this way.

All of which leaves me a little bit troubled. We're all familiar with the obvious issues—sexual harassment, exploitation, favoritism, and so on. But it seems to me that we are far less aware of the severe dysfunctions caused by too much "friendship" at work. Such as:

- Poor morale
- Mistrust
- Miscommunication or lack of communication
- Poor decision-making
- Inability to hold people accountable
- Outright favoritism

Google, a top global brand and a most-sought-after employer as well, has considered emotional bonds as part of its quest to build the ideal team. As reported by the *New York Times*, it's found that a certain amount of emotional openness is a good thing at work. It promotes trust, which helps create a sense of safety that employees badly need in order to work productively.

45

5 Telltale Signs Your Office Culture Is a Problem

Think of corporate culture as the human spine. If it's well-formed and agile, it supports the body well over time; if it's bent out of shape inside, the body winds up in enormous and constant pain.Unfortunately, when an organization is misaligned, the pain is felt not only companywide but also by its individual employees. So no matter what your role in your own organization, here are 5 things to look for to assess its level of health. If something is out of whack, it pays to prepare yourself in advance for managing the symptoms that will inevitably come up:

- **Decision-making:** A framework of principles, informed by a constant stream of data, is a healthy way to plot a course of action. It is not healthy to delay decisions interminably or to use arbitrary, gut-based, person-based, situational "I just feel like it" reasoning.
- **Empowerment:** Define the job accurately, hire people who can do the job and who play well with others, and

then let them do their job. If you're second-guessing them every minute, you may as well fire them and save the money.

- **Prioritization:** Yes you have a lot of things to do and a lot of emails within which to discuss those things. Not all of those things are equally important. Dump most of it and there will be absolutely zero impact to your productivity. An organization that refuses or fails to prioritize and instead categorizes busywork as productivity is an organization that is trying to engage in empire-building rather than the delivery of value to the customer.
- **Attitude:** We are excited to be here. We have a great team. We are here to improve, we can improve and we will improve without fail. This is the way work should be approached every single second of every day. A culture of negativity, gossip, complaining, and rumination about why things will never get better is a culture that drags otherwise positive people down into a pit. That pit will swallow innovation whole.
- **Meetings:** They should be relatively short and oriented at engaging people in a discussion. Attendees need to know the agenda in advance and do their homework beforehand. If some people are sitting around picking their noses and playing with their iPhones under the desk while other people are droning on, then something is wrong.

Of course, it goes without saying that you should not try to fix any or all of these problems on your own. As a sociologist with nearly 20 years of studying organizations both formally and informally, I can tell you that this is a recipe for workplace suicide. What you can do, though, is model a healthier way;

call out the contradictions between the company's espoused ideals and the ones it is practicing. Over time, as you quietly demonstrate consistent productivity, others will follow your example.

46

Do You Really Know Who You're Dealing With?

I accepted a new position last week that will involve, once again, being a supervisor.

I've been preparing for the role by asking seasoned managers for their input on how to hit the ground running, and for 360 degree type feedback about their perceptions of me at work. You can never ask enough.

As I walked past the desk of an administrative assistant with whom I am friendly, I asked if I could "interview" her. It took about thirty seconds to realize that I was talking to someone with extensive managerial experience, in both the military and in the private sector.

For months, she had seemed to belong to a certain category, but after all this time it was clear: I didn't know who I was dealing with.

Many of us naturally categorize people this way, but branding has made us even worse. We've become accustomed to making quick decisions. We need to because we all suffer from information overload. It's much easier to think: *Look at the shoes, she must be rich. Look at his coat, he must be poor.* And then subtly adjust our reactions accordingly.

Remember the movie "Trading Places," with Eddie Murphy and Dan Akroyd? Eddie was a con artist and Dan was a spoiled an incompetent rich kid, until each assumed the position of the other. Or "Freaky Friday" — the original, with Jodie Foster, and the remake, with Lindsay Lohan and Jamie Lee Curtis. Mom and daughter switch bodies, but nobody else knows.

Remember Big, with Tom Hanks? That piano scene in FAO Schwartz?

You never, *never* know who you're dealing with.

It's said frequently: The person who's your colleague today may tomorrow be your boss.

You knew that. But how often do you really think about this principle in everyday life?

In the hall I told a normally quiet colleague about my new position.

"I knew it already," he said.

"How did you know that? I didn't even tell you," I answered.

"Because you were disinterested last week. It was in the air."

Do you realize how closely you are being observed? Do you know who is observing you? Do you respect the depth of their perception?

At the nursing home where we used to visit my husband's mom, the residents had private rooms. Each room had a shadowbox on the outside with personal photos and a memento, whatever the residents chose to put there.

It was easy to dismiss those shadowboxes because they were small and they tended to look the same. Who would stop and inspect someone else's unfamiliar pictures?

But one woman had her entire door plastered with newspaper clippings. These were impossible to ignore. They lauded her career as a decorated military veteran, the first to do this and the most accomplished at that.

One time I peeked inside, just a little, to see who this woman was. She was small and skinny. I couldn't see her face but her body was inanimate.

In the lunchroom I wouldn't have picked this woman out of the crowd. But I knew Mom, and why she was so special to me.

I don't know you, and you don't know me.

Don't assume anything about anyone.

47

Please Don't Talk About THAT

Many times, I hear people say things like: "you can talk about this and can talk about that, but please don't talk about that."

I remember when I was a little girl and whenever a controversial subject came up my mother used to say "shhh" and her mother used to say "shhh" and my other grandmother used to say the same. Generally everyone said "shhh" to keep the peace.

As an adult this comes up all the time. When you're dealing with your kids' school and there is an issue, you don't want to antagonize the teacher or the principal. When you're at work and there is a difficult issue, you don't want to antagonize your boss. And, of course, in your relationship when a difficult issue comes up you don't want to antagonize your partner.

But I was reading this good article about the Google way of solving problems — which is to "attack" them — and it reminded me of something I have learned over time. The only way to truly tackle a difficult issue is to have everybody talk about it pretty much openly, without anyone being told to "keep your mouth shut," whether implicitly or explicitly, especially nowadays when we have so many problems to solve. We just don't have time for this kind of nonsense.

One other point. I have had the experience of going from environments where you weren't supposed to talk, to those where you were encouraged to contribute every idea that could help to address an issue. And it was an amazing feeling to be treated as though all opinions were valuable.

What I saw was that when the level of trust and respect in a group is high, it is possible to share conflicting points of view and even to disagree on things that can only be resolved through someone making a decision that the other person will never agree with. The decision can be made and everyone can agree to disagree and simply finish the job and go about their day, it isn't taken personally and it doesn't leave a lasting wound.

Stifling conversation clamping down on conflict and otherwise trying to control the conversation is so 20th century, so "Organization Man." It's time to embrace a new paradigm where everybody gets to have their say.

48

The #1 Dysfunction Preventing Wise Investment In Employee Engagement

You SAY you are bothered by the fact that employees are "checked-out."

You CLAIM you want them to innovate.

You DISCUSS over and over the fact that they just seem to sit there, taking up space, not doing nearly as much as they could or should.

But what, exactly, are you DOING about it?

The fact of the matter is that at any given time, most of the people working for you are doing exactly what you're worried they're doing: sitting there, underutilized and under-motivated, thinking about how soon they can log out, go home and get their sanity back.

You know this. You don't need to see yet another survey confirming this fact, do you?

And you say you want to do something about it. Maybe you really do, who knows: You're willing to consider their requests for a training class, after all.

But it's not clear to me that you REALLY want to motivate

your staff, after all.

Because if you did, you would ACTUALLY do something about it.

You don't do anything, even though you know – or you should know – that employees are more than your greatest asset. In reality, they are your ONLY asset.

The reason you hang back, to be honest, is fear. You don't want to know what would happen if they did actually get engaged.

Maybe they'd end up firing me and taking over.

That is a very scary thought, right there. And you can't admit that you're afraid. Of course!

That's why fear is a HIDDEN dysfunction.

So you make up the most logical business reason of all to keep your staff from succeeding: money.

- "We can't afford for you to take that class."
- "We can't afford for you to be out of the office."
- "We can't afford for you to stop doing all the other stuff you're doing and learn something not 100% related to your current job."

What I want to tell you, if you're even remotely in a position to help employees get engaged, is that these fears are not only unfounded.

They're actually KEEPING you, the supervisor, from progressing ahead in your career.

Consider this: A manager who helps employees gain developmental opportunities is BELOVED by them.

That means your staff are LOYAL to you, SUPPORTIVE of you, in SYNC with you, ENGAGED with the work they're doing for you, and most importantly of all, they TRUST you.

That's the first thing to know.

The second is that there are PLENTY of ways they can gain experience at absolutely zero cost to you. If that is truly what you're afraid of. They can:

1. Get a mentor, inside or outside the organization.
2. Be a mentor themselves.
3. Do a rotation somewhere else in the company or agency.
4. Do a detail outside the agency, part-time or temporarily.
5. Join a working group.
6. Attend class at a community college.
7. Take on a leadership position in a related organization.
8. Engage in low-cost online training.
9. Teach themselves material with which to train other employees.
10. And if you're brave – you can delegate some work to them that they are naturally talented at, but which they lack the skills to complete on their own.

Think about it: People have a natural survival instinct. Instead of fearing it, and trying to smash it down and destroy it, why don't you work with it instead?

Believe me, the stuff I'm telling you here – I didn't make it up on my own. Not at all.

I learned it from brilliant managers, the ones I've had who really understood the way to get the most out of their team.

The philosophy can be summed up in a single sentence, uttered more than a decade ago by one such individual, a chief of staff at an agency within the U.S. Department of the Treasury:

"The pie gets bigger the more you share it."

Consider the source: This is a person who should naturally say the opposite. After all, how can you split a dollar in half?

But he understood that power, like wealth, is never actually in limited supply. That in fact, these things exist not only in substance but in the mind.

And that generosity from the one has an actual physical effect on the other.

That oddly, giving away has an additive effect (or even multiplying) rather than subtracting.

That in the end, helping OTHER PEOPLE to succeed is the best way to boost your career after all.

49

On Creating A "Less Miserable" Work Environment

With the growth of products like Yammer, Jive, Socialtext, and even instant messaging at work, the whole conversation is becoming irrelevant.

The power of a superior (leaders, manager, supervisor) to create a lousy work environment is directly correlated with their ability to shut people up. More specifically the power to stop people from forming groups where mistreatment is openly aired (you could never really stop people from having one on one conversations offline).

Older folks like us are just starting to grasp this premise. But the younger generation is very intuitive about it. They have no problem marching into a classroom, an office, anywhere really and taping what's going on then posting it online.

(As I recently learned when I lost my temper with my daughter, and she taped me on her iPhone, then played it back for my husband! Yes – that actually happened and I was mortified!)

Once people find out who is good to work for, which

department is good to work for, which agency is good to work for, what's going on in the private sector vs. the public sector, etc. the system will correct itself. For survival's sake, leaders will have to adapt to the empowered workforce.

The empowerment of employees is something I care a lot about. As a communicator with a lot of background in internal communications and organizational development it has frequently been depressing to see the gap between what we say to the outside world, and how we treat people on the inside.

(And sometimes fulfilling – because of leaders and non-leaders who have integrity and really treat people with heart – the problem being that as a rule they never want credit or publicity for it at all and are horrified when you suggest it.)

I was watching Joel Osteen on TV a couple of weeks ago and he talked about salvation arriving "suddenly." It is my feeling that the moment of salvation for employees has arrived, thanks to G-d's infinite mercy in providing us the tools of the Internet and social media.

50

Internal & External Messaging At The Government Agency: Together or Separate?

It's hard to give advice, because there is no one right way – culture determines the answer to most of these questions. That said, I've worked in four government agencies and in each, internal communication was taken seriously and kept very separate from public affairs or external messaging.

This is because employees tend to be concerned about 1) leadership/management/how best to approach the mission 2) career advancement, pay, benefits 3) climate of fairness. They are also very wired-in and know a lot about what's going on, so messages aimed at the public are likely too generic.

On the other hand, the public tends to care about 1) how well agency is managed, stewardship of taxpayer funds 2) accountability, transparency, efficiency 3) very specific hot button issues. They also may want datasets, which are not a focus for employees.

For reasons most of us can probably guess, I've rarely

seen corporate or agency internal communication be truly engaging. If it is, it's spontaneous rather than planned. Real communication provokes emotion, and emotion can be dangerous.

This part I did not say:

As far as intranets go, I believe they are less and less meaningful and should ideally be consolidated with a social networking environment. The aspect of the information that is non-sensitive can go on the public website, while other information can be published in a social, collaborative space.

XI

Leadership

51

Lead, Follow or Get Out Of The Way

Once I worked with a career counselor who gave me some great advice: "Try to think of work as an anthropology experiment," she said to me. "Observe the people like you've embarked on a field trip, and write down what you see."

It was the best advice anybody ever gave me, not just about coping with an unpredictable and stressful work environment, but generally about coping with life. If you can observe yourself and write down what you are feeling, or capture it in some other way (for example, drawing or photography or music) then despite your actual lack of control over many things, you perceive yourself as empowered because at the very least your experiences matter, you're telling your story, and it is your story to tell.

There is a reason they call work "work," and that is the fact that normally it is stressful. When I first started working in government, at a different agency than I work at right now, I participated in a significant reorganization. Naturally, people were upset about it.

But we had a gifted chief of staff. In response to concerns

that people would lose out professionally because of the reorg, he said, "Do not worry about dividing the pie. The pie gets bigger when you share."

Supporting the chief of staff was my boss's boss, the director of communications. He was talking to us in a staff meeting one day, and as I recall he was talking about organizational change. "The train is leaving the station," he said. "You've got to get on the train."

Now I am the granddaughter of Holocaust survivors, my grandmother (may she rest in peace) was at Auschwitz, and so when I hear about "the train leaving the station" some terrible intergenerational trauma is unleashed. So I don't like that phrase.

But I can relate to "get on the bus," as in, "the organization is moving in a certain direction, and you can express your views all you want before the decision is made, but once it is made you either have to join up and execute or find another place to work."

Which brings me to the present day. A few weeks ago, I took an excellent training course where we learned what it means to be a great staff officer. One of the most fundamental things I took away from this course was the importance of supporting a decision once it has been made—whether or not you agree with it. This isn't to say that you can't have your opinions, and even share them, but there is a time and a place and limit for everything.

I am the most skeptical, questioning person in the world. But at the end of the day, the team cannot support endless griping and negativity."

"Say what you have to say," my mother used to say, "and then let's get on with business."

52

Want Innovation? 10 Tips for Senior Leaders

You can help your staff to wildly succeed. Here are some ideas that may be helpful.

1. **You rely on your staff to do the work for you. Let them.** Don't micromanage their work. Don't act like you know their job better than they do. Make a decision. Make a phone call on their behalf. Make things work in their favor, make the system work for them. Give them ground cover with the higher-ups. Make it possible for staff to wildly succeed, just because of you.
2. **Do not take credit for staff work. Ever.** When someone says to you, "That XYZ initiative sure took off like a shot," respond back to them, "It was Jane Doe's idea, isn't she marvelous?"
3. **Speaking of ideas: When someone comes to you and says, "I have an idea," immediately say, "Go for it!"** Even if you have to do it as a modified pilot with no funds, undertaken on 10 percent training time.

4. **Here is what you should not say when someone has an idea: "That's a great idea, but it will never work. Thanks so very much for trying."** Please do not ever use the word "impossible."

5. **If you asked for advanced education and experience in the job announcement, draw on it.** Why are you treating a GS-13 like a GS-5?

6. **Understand that innovation means one or more of the following: "breaking the rules," "ignoring the rules," "doing things differently," "paying no attention to the past."** Stop saying you want innovation, but rewarding conformists in practice.

7. **Innovation involves a lot of trial and error. So when someone makes a mistake, don't define their entire career by the error.** As in: "There goes John Doe. Remember him? He totally messed up that launch in FY13, and now he works in the basement."

8. **Stop playing favorites.** People who brownnose you are relying on their smarmy skills to get ahead, not their actual expertise. And do you know what? One day they'll be brownnosing somebody else, and you'll be mopping floors.

9. **Speaking of culture, don't tolerate groupthink.** It's not the same thing as "people getting along." It is born of a culture of repression, and a culture of repression is negatively correlated with a culture of results. Remember you'll have to answer for what you did each fiscal year — and justify that enormous salary. If you want those good metrics, you'll have to embrace painful truth wherever you hear it.

10. **Learn to love social.** It's been around for a while and

it hasn't broken the government yet. If you want that magical word "collaboration" to happen, you are going to have to get over it. And you'll have to do all those "soft, squishy" things that aren't operational, too — like open a customer service desk, and actually wish your employees "happy birthday." Remember that people mostly remember how you made them feel, not what you actually did. And that is true whether you're working one-on-one with a staffer, or rolling out a new program to hundreds of millions of people at once.

53

Why Top Executives Keep Employees in The Dark

Have you ever noticed that most organizations don't spend a lot of time telling you how they get things done?

Typically, very little information is available explicitly:

- Our management guru of choice: Is it Steve Jobs, Jack Welch, Tom Peters, Peter Drucker, or someone else? What books do we read, what discipline do we follow?
- The history, mission and current challenges facing the organization: When did it get started? What were the meaningful moments? Who do we revere here? What difference did they make? What do we need to do now, and why?
- The little things: When people go to lunch. How to address superiors (first name only or more formally?), send emails (short or long, or maybe we usually talk in person), and so on?
- The brass tacks: What are our standard operating procedures? How do we define each job? Your job? When we

sit down together at the end of the year and talk about a bonus, will you have known all this time what you could have done to earn it?

No matter how sophisticated your operation, only human beings can get the work done. Only people can make the decisions, pull the levers, and leverage the technologies. So why do we leave them grasping for answers in the dark?

I think the answer is that the higher they go up the food chain, the less executives understand how very little most people in the organization know. That's because they are having conversations at the top. Most executives not only don't understand the downstream impact of ignorance, they actually do not see, and cannot understand, that it exists.

But they do see that employees are unmotivated, that they don't care.

Here's a good way to fix that problem: Tell people what is going on, what you want from them, and how they can help. In short:

> *"A company is people ... employees want to know...*
> *am I being listened to or am I a cog in the wheel?*
> *People really need to feel wanted."* — *Richard Branson,*
> *Founder, Virgin Enterprises*

You don't have to make a big deal out of "internal communication" programs or hire a huge specialized staff to speak in a foreign language to those you manage. Just step back and let them do what they are supposed to do in the first place.

If you don't, guess what is going to happen?

They will "divorce" you.

But before they leave, they'll be disengaged, pushing email back and forth, getting into needless conflicts with other employees, and eventually marking time while they find another employer that loves and values them.

Of course, there are many intelligently run organizations out there. They make sure that staff members know their place on the team, that they're up to speed, formally and informally.

Here's Richard Branson again:

> *"Complexity is your enemy. Any fool can make something complicated. It is hard to keep things simple."*

In fact, great organizations go well beyond informing. Their focus is on marketing, and they market from top to bottom and all the way back up again because they know that employees are really all they have in terms of assets. With every word, every assignment, every email and every chat they communicate:

> *"You were born to be a player. You were meant to be here. This moment is yours." — Herb Brooks (1937–2003), head coach of the extraordinary 1980 U.S. Olympic hockey team*

54

How Well Are the Bosses Bossing?

It's that time of year again. Time to do your annual self-rating and submit it to your boss, after which time you have a performance discussion, and after that you get a report card that you have to sign.

Personally I find the whole process utterly painful. Somewhat inefficient. Incomplete. Even degrading.

The real performance discussions happen all year round (or they don't), and you know what your boss is looking for from you. You know that you do well on some of those fronts, but certainly not all. It's like marriage: You may be the most devoted spouse in the world but then again you are the most irritating one, too. Especially when you leave the cap off the toothpaste, no matter how many times they tell you to put it back on.

(For me it's the damn Outlook calendar.)

You know and your boss knows that there's a whole thicket of issues around writing the formal performance appraisal, and you do this dance — saying and not saying, thinking and they're thinking — and the result is, well, it is something. It's not clear what it is, but the words look like English written on a page.

A really good performance appraisal helps you, for sure. It's a piece of paper that says to somebody else: Hey, this person did a good job there, they've got value as an employee. Hire them.

You know that, and so does your boss.

Conversely, a bad performance appraisal, or even one that is nonchalant, doesn't do very much for your career — obviously.

So you really want that piece of paper to be good.

But you also want it to be honest. You do a lot of work during the year that the boss doesn't see, work outside of your strict performance requirements probably, work that you innovated and which may or may not have seen a reward.

You want recognition. You want some respect. You want the people in charge to value you.

It's hard to say what motivates your boss. Maybe they care about your professional development. Maybe they're devoted to honesty and integrity, and want to capture something accurate about your positives and negatives as a staffer. Certainly they don't have a lot of time, because they have to do actual work in addition to managing you. And they don't want to have to argue later on about whether the appraisal was fair, or worse, get into a legal tangle.

There is also the larger system to think of, of course: Both you and your supervisor are situated in a complicated web of reporting requirements. The paperwork has to be in on time, no matter what state of perfection it's in.

And the other thing. Nowhere in the system are you actually

rating your supervisor.

Nowhere in the system is the supervisor pledging to perform against certain management metrics, and assigning key performance indicators and weights to those.

As a result, they can be the worst, most abusive, most arbitrary and incompetent boss alive, and nobody on the planet is going to know it, other than if you sink your career by making a stink.

So performance appraisals don't help organizational productivity much. At best, they provide a partial picture of employee performance. At worst, they misrepresent reality, create ill will between employee and supervisor, and entrench poor performers in place, while totally ignoring a critical question: How well are the bosses bossing the employees?

Obviously, this question is a critical one if our greatest asset is our people, as we are frequently wont to say.

If I had a magic wand, I would eliminate performance appraisals entirely and substitute instead six quantitative "pulse" surveys a year, followed by appointments to have real conversations. Employees would rate supervisors anonymously. Supervisors would rate employees one at a time, and they would have to provide at least one sentence of explanatory information after any highly positive or negative rating.

The result of these conversations would be rolled up into an annual review, which would be relatively automatic and based on the previous conversations.

It isn't a perfect suggestion I'm offering. But I think it would get us closer to whatever representation of reality one might call "the truth."

XII

Management

55

Restoring Health to a Civil Service on Life Support

To hear some senior executives tell it, the federal civil service is on life support, and its pulse grows weaker by the day. Without a sufficient number of skilled employees to oversee the effective functioning of the government, our nation suffers myriad security risks, not to mention the silent but deadly cancer of waste, fraud and abuse, a disease which inevitably grows to consume the body unless it is stopped early on.

The research comes from the nonprofit Senior Executives Association, and it points to a number of risk factors that may ultimately tear the civil service apart.

Most fundamentally, there aren't enough people to do all the inherently governmental work required to serve the American people: In 1960, there were 180.67 million of us; by December 2018, that number had nearly doubled, to 329.10 million. Yet according to the study, from 1960-2017, the civil service barely increased in number—from 1.8 to 2.1 million federal workers.

You might be thinking that this shrunken workforce is no big deal, because contractors can pick up the slack. And surely they have, at least to some extent: According to USASpending.gov, in 2018, the federal government spent $200 billion on contracts.

The problem, however, is that for the government to function properly, it has to limit what contractors can do, because some functions are by law inherently governmental. To oversimplify it, these include, but are not limited to decisions about:

- Contracts
- Military or diplomatic action
- Civil or criminal judicial proceedings
- Decisions that "significantly" have an impact on "the life, liberty, or property interests of private persons"
- Hiring people
- Managing U.S. money or property.

From a financial point of view, what might seem like an easy fix—having a flexible, even disposable workforce that grows and shrinks depending on need—quickly mushrooms into a nightmare. It is not illegal to seek to make a profit, and as profit-seeking entities, contractors will embed themselves into the fabric of the organizational culture.

The report also notes that citizens' expectations of government have increased with the proliferation of digital tools. People expect a higher level of service than in the past, and with the Internet, a 24/7/365 mindset has become the norm. While nobody is suggesting that we should pay people to read email, the reality is that someone has to keep the business of government going and answer the concerns of the people. Doing so requires a ceaseless process of reading and absorbing information, and responding quickly and accurately.

The report goes on to note that robots may well be able to do the work that people once did. But while these technologies may be useful in some settings, the reality is that they aren't quite "there" yet, and the civil servant is in fact needed to administer the functions of government, in emergencies and ordinary times alike.

We could recite a laundry list of "things civil servants do," but the bottom line is that decimating the federal workforce while padding the pockets of contractors is unlikely to result in value for the taxpayer.

Covering this story for *Government Executive*, Erich Wagner highlights some other findings. First, and most troublingly, "work overload" combined with poor performance management (read: lots of punishment, few rewards) means that the federal workforce is "fatally risk averse and as a result chooses inaction to action during critical times."

Obviously this is a dangerous situation, because an employee who is not empowered to handle a complex, sensitive, evolving and murky situation with good judgment is not just useless but dangerous.

The second issue has to do with the way in which political partisanship has infected the civil service through political appointees' pervasive suspicion of career civil servants. The study's authors are careful to note that this is not a partisan issue—the problem has grown increasingly worse since the 1980's—but that it has become more noxious as "each change in administration is like a hostile corporate takeover."

What's to be done? Of course we can sit around moaning

and groaning about the problems we face, or we can try to fix them.

- With respect to the partisanship problem, one simple but powerful approach might be to revisit the notion of "bridge-building," finding common ground between people whose vastly different world views are rooted in the same underlying desire to serve. (If someone actually has another agenda in mind, that is a different problem, one that will not be resolved here.)

- In terms of excessive spending, it would be useful for government to clearly explain to citizens where their money is going, without a proliferation of confusing spending dashboards and tools. The misperception over over-spending on civil servants comes directly from conflating contractor spend with salary spend in reports such as this one from the Government Accountability Office, which resulted in numerous headlines decrying the wasted $1.5 billion per year spent on "public relations."

- Finally, a third area to be addressed is the impact of many civil service retirements at once, which gnaws a hole directly in the institutional knowledge base of a body of employees that does not necessarily have all its information housed in an accessible way. While one can cynically say that many long-time civil servants are part of the problem, the reality is that their knowledge makes the difference between a program that is legal, sensible and smoothly implemented and one that crashes and burns upon arrival. As new employees join up, they can and should be trained cross-functionally, and further trained on the emerging technologies that make it possible to operate effectively with a relatively lean staff.

As a civil servant, one of the most rewarding things about my job is the appreciation people share when they receive the service their hard-earned taxpayer dollars have paid for. It would be a shame if nonstop fighting left our country bereft of the body of decent, hardworking people who make that service a reality.

56

Five Ways To Be A Clueless Manager

Your job is to get the work done, partially on your own but mostly through leveraging the talent of other people.

Here's where you may be screwing up (and nobody's going stick their neck out and tell you):

You don't understand your job very well. It's not about keeping the trains moving on time. It's about making sure the trains are safe. If the staff is doing stupid busywork, change the work.

You jump to conclusions. A manager is the hub between staff and leadership. Both sides have a point of view. If you act like Gilligan and simply accept what people tell you, or worse, make up your mind before finding out the facts, whatever you do next will be misguided.

You don't pay attention to the larger political climate. There are ideas, words, groups and people who are in favor, and conversely, there are those who are on the outs. If you try to handle a work team in isolation from these intangible but very real facts, guess how effective your efforts will be? Additionally, you have to deal with the very real fact that the organization itself is likely fractured and dysfunctional, and that the problems in your division, office or work team are a symptom of that impossible-for-you-to-change reality.

You refuse to think critically about people's motives. This isn't to say that your colleagues are "bad." It is to say that each person operates from a locus of self-interest. What is it that people want out of a situation? What evidence do you have of the drivers behind their behavior? It is your job to understand those things as best you can. Otherwise, you are driving blind on the freeway.

You are afraid to admit when you're out of your league. Everybody has limitations. Take me. I have social anxiety, believe it or not. Also vertigo. So if you tell me I have to go to a party and drive for an hour to get there, I am going to fight the whole situation like a cat, because that's me. We all face situations like that at work—triggers, issues, fears, situations we just aren't skilled at handling. Instead of being defensive, that is precisely the time to go to your boss or someone else you trust to help you, and lay it all out.

Many people think that management is an outdated job and that marshaling talent forward is a "layer" of the organization that is becoming less and less necessary.

But from where I sit as a practicing manager, this profession and these skills are more important than ever. The problem is only that we don't properly understand—or take the time to learn—the dimensions of what it is we are supposed to be doing.

57

Managers Need to Edit Themselves Before Taking On Subordinates

Once there was this senior executive—okay, he was the head of my huge law enforcement agency—who really, *really* took writing to heart.

Every month I gave him a draft column for the magazine. And every month he sent it back to me (I could almost hear him huffing and puffing) with a plethora of scrawled edits: "NO! NO! NO!"

Another executive used to simply take the draft and rewrite the whole thing, every time, well past the deadline.

Senior executives live and die by the power of their communication. They can only really delegate to someone who thinks exactly like themselves. As David Samuels discovered about President Obama and his chief communicator, Ben Rhodes:

> *Part of what accounts for Rhodes's influence is his "mind meld" with the president. Nearly everyone I spoke to about Rhodes used the phrase "mind meld" verbatim....He doesn't think for the president, but he*

knows what the president is thinking, which is a source of tremendous power. One day, when Rhodes and I were sitting in his boiler-room office, he confessed, with a touch of bafflement, "I don't know anymore where I begin and Obama ends." - David Samuels, " The Aspiring Novelist Who Became President Obama's Foreign Policy Guru," The New York Times Magazine, May 5, 2016

Most of us writers are not Ben Rhodes, though. So we actually need our senior executives to be extremely involved—to focus on the message itself, while trusting us to make their words clear and engaging.

But communication is only one part of a much larger issue when it comes to effectively running an organization: How much should supervisory professionals "edit" the work of their subordinates?

Think about how confusing this is. On the one hand, we are encouraged to empower people. But on the other, we insist on holding leaders and managers accountable for results, even when we aren't exactly sure what "results" actually means.

Plus there is pressure, when you're in a management role, to "prove" that you are adding some value to the organization. If your employees are doing just fine without your red pencil editorial reviews, then what exactly are we paying you for?

But it's not good management to constantly be in people's faces. And subordinates should not need to be mind readers to do a good job.

Can you imagine if we ran the Army this way? "Oh we don't have standard operating procedures," we'd say to new recruits. "Just do what I do, and you can repeat my opinions after me."

People wouldn't last very long on the battlefield.

It seems to me that the job of a manager is in fact the opposite of what one might think: To make sure that people can normally do their work independently. Ideally, enable them to innovate, so that they waste less time and get a lot more done. This isn't abdicating the role, but rather being so skillful about how you perform it that it looks like you almost aren't there.

Here's an interesting parallel from the world of makeup. It turns out that women are perceived as significantly more attractive when we wear subtle cosmetics. Overdone makeup takes away from a woman's beauty, and no makeup whatsoever does nothing to enhance it.

So we need the subtle manager in our lives, the kind that if it were a lipstick would be called "natural": In the background, behind the scenes but present, constantly monitoring, evaluating, adjusting, and enhancing the output of the work unit.

But we don't need, and can't afford, the "cherry red" version: ranting and raving, self-important, sadistic, and ultimately incompetent version.

Not the take-out-your-red-pencil, make-her-feel-stupid, nobody-can-get-a-thing-done-without-me kind of manager.

Not the demoralizing, disempowering, devaluing, and degrading one, who makes themselves look good by putting others down in comparison.

Even if you're supervising writers, there's a better way to help them generate communication than to insist they read the boss's mind. I've heard that complaint from people more than once, and they shouldn't have to do that to be rated outstanding any more than they should have to stay late, make coffee, buy drinks or form a personal friendship with the boss.

When I first became a manager I asked my husband for advice.

"Don't bother people," he said. "If you can remember that, the rest will come naturally."

58

Why You Should Squash the Urge to Quash Those Who Disagree

In recent months I've had to de-friend a number of people on Facebook. I enjoy hearing diverse views but it has degenerated to this:

"Well I know where you get your news."

"The fact that you could even say that means you aren't worth debating."

"You need help."

"That comment is beneath you."

"You're an ignorant idiot schmuck."

How has civil discourse sunk to such low levels? A great article by Sean Blanda, "The 'Other Side' Is Not Dumb," explains it in terms of psychology, the "false-consensus bias." Essentially we are confounded when other people show signs that they don't think the same way we do.

On social media, being confronted by different viewpoints leads us to assume the worst. If you don't agree with me - well then you must be crazy!

> *"We and our friends are the sane ones and . . . there's a crazy Other Side that must be laughed at — an Other Side that just doesn't get it, and is clearly not as intelligent as us."*

The problem with allowing the "false consensus bias" to proliferate, says Blanda, is that we lose out on the opportunity to actually learn something from those who vehemently disagree with our views.

"If we want to consider online discourse productive, we need to move past this."

As Blanda rightly points out, it is important that we preserve the civic town hall that is Facebook and other forms of online conversation. That is a social need. And it is important for each of us to practice listening, not just preaching, in these forums.

But there is another problem here that must be pointed out as well. When the virtual world becomes a place of forced consensus, those with dissenting views are essentially shut down from airing their unique and valuable points of view.

This can happen in a lot of ways. It can take the form of direct, rude comments as above. But it can also happen in other ways.

- Shock: "You're supporting who? Really?"
- Expressions of concern for you, when you begin sharing news about social ills that really make people uncomfortable: "Don't you think it's a little too much?"

Sometimes people are actually supportive: "Thank you for sharing that," they might say. Or you see that they've shared your post with others. That is the good side of an online interchange.

I've been part of conversation that changed my own views about the world. Politically, religiously, culturally, psychologically. Whether it's others who have completely different views, or respectful disagreement where the flaws in one's argument are pointed to and countered. Those are the most fruitful conversations of all.

One thing I know. You will never get squashed sharing a personal anecdote or funny statistic; a photo of your family at a family barbecue; cat videos; peace mantras; or anything with Kim Kardashian and/or Taylor Swift. Those topics are safe.

But is that really all there is, safety?

For your sake, and our sake, the world that depends on your uniqueness, please do not be a sheep.

Whether other people like it or not, we all need to hear what you're thinking.

59

Reinventing Management, Again

In 1994, Peter Drucker gave a lecture to government employees called "Reinventing Government: The Next Phase." (The Drucker Lectures, 2010)

In it, he commented on the National Partnership for Reinventing Government, earlier known as the National Performance Review and commonly known as NPR. This was a governmentwide management reform initiative spearheaded by Al Gore, which led to the founding of the Federal Communicators Network 20 years ago. (I previously served as Chair of the FCN from 2011-2012.)

Drucker praises NPR's success, crediting the fact that it was "focused on performance." However, he shares his concern that an "individual, isolated" change effort is "just good intentions unless it becomes permanent, organized, self-generated habit."

Ultimately NPR had a significant impact, including $137 billion in savings. But Drucker's concerns were well-placed, as the work of the NPR influenced future administrations, but was not duplicated by them in the same way.

At its height NPR made a tangible positive difference in the way government functioned, not only because it was an interagency entity but also because it was well-funded and well-staffed, with 250 federal employees paid by their home agencies all working together.

Warned Drucker:

> *"We need 'reinventing government.' If we do not make a start on it, then pretty soon we face catastrophe within the next 10 years or so . . . The danger here is very great that government will be exposed to something very similar to what has happened in a lot of big companies. I call it "amputation without diagnosis."*

If we know what to do and how to do it, is it necessary to reinvent the wheel?

The forthcoming FCN white paper, "Advancing Federal Communications," makes the argument for integration from a communications standpoint.

But such integration is only doable when there exists an integrated approach toward managing the government enterprise overall.

<h1 style="text-align:center">60</h1>

I Hate Meetings And They Stink

I have had this happen to me SO many times.

I'm sitting in a meeting, and something is going on. Not something like an actual thing, but a tense, negative, or unproductive social dynamic between two people or within the group. I must be like The Terminator of sociology because I can actually sense these situations, like in the movie where the heat-seeking goggles glowed red when there were humans around.

Bad vibes like this are why I usually hate meetings. Particularly because people are generally averse to working out conflict openly, so I have to watch it and not talk while it's actually going on. Just sit there and have to wait it out till it's over and I can be real again.

Here are some examples beyond the usual Blackberry/smartphone/cellphone abuse:

1. Asserting, without explanation, that an idea will definitely not work
2. Completely ignoring a suggestion and going on to the

next person

3. Making the "are you crazy?" face
4. Rolling eyeballs behind someone's back
5. Responding to idea with blank stare/silence
6. Ganging up on someone (meeting their suggestion with two "no's")
7. Laughing at someone's ideas
8. Standing up and leaving the meeting without explanation
9. Going into "deep chair slouch"
10. Closing eyes

True, sometimes I find myself entertained by the goings on. Sometimes I hear things that are funny, or the group gets along and there are decent jokes. Always there is some gossip, that's not too bad. Meetings can be educational as well, seriously. But more often than not, as soon as they get into full swing I feel like I am 9 years old again and watching a big family dinner degenerate.

Please don't start writing comments about how YOUR place of work has fantastic meetings and how you feel bad for me, OK? It's not about any particular agency; I've been around for more than a dozen years, both in government and outside it, and they all generally stink. As soon as you call it a "meeting" and whip out the leather portfolios and play business card roulette, group dynamics start going into motion and the pain begins.

I actually did have a good meeting recently. I had to participate in a phone call to plan for another meeting (yes, this is Washington, land of meetings) and to be honest I had dreaded the phone call all morning. Not because of the participants, but just because I get nervous about planned social interactions. Surprise, surprise. My skin is about as thick as wax paper.

Then, mercifully, the whole thing lasted maybe 15 minutes. Fortunately for me most of the other participants did not remember to get on the call! And those of us that remained agreed: We were so relieved not to have to continue the meeting and everything would work out just fine and we would immediately get back to our cubes, or Starbucks or whatever place we could go to with our notebooks and hide from the rest of humanity to recover.

Actually, wait. I have to admit that I had another good meeting today. And that is because the vendor forgot to show up. We all sat around waiting for awhile until it was clear that we had been stood up, and it couldn't properly be called a meeting anymore. That was when the dynamics stopped and we started to just be ourselves.

Maybe the problem with meetings is that we associate them with the pressure to seem like a grownup, when inside we're all just little kids. We think that grownups at meetings have to show up and seem to know some amazing, mystical important thing. Like the meeting room is a gladiator ring, and our brains and smart mouths are our weapons. And if we don't show up and fight, we're dead.

And then there's all this talk about being collaborative! And we're surprised when people are not!

I wonder what life would be like at meetings if we forgot that we were at work. We could imagine that work is over, that it's happy hour or back in college or even back to the days of our childhood, when we sat outside and waited on the porch for the ice cream truck.

My mother told me yesterday that some rabbits gave birth on her front lawn and the neighborhood girls hung around to watch as my mom figured out how to deal with it. I'm sure they gave her advice too. Maybe it was kind of a – meeting – because surely my mom called the neighbors and they all weighed in.

I know this sounds totally disgusting, the whole rabbits giving birth part, but I have a feeling that the rabbit meeting was sort of cool. Because the getting together was not about a fight to the death but rather about actually hanging out together and solving a problem too. Which is really what meetings should be about.

Elderly people know how to have meetings too. I see them sometimes hanging around in packs. Comparing notes, complaining, yakking away the time.

Funny how kids and the elderly seem to understand a paradox of time: how it can at once seem to stretch out endlessly and be just about gone. It's not that they aren't ever hostile to each other, just that they either haven't learned or have gotten past the need to aggressively prove themselves by excluding or being hostile to others.

I say we get rid of meetings altogether and replace them with potluck lunches, vegan. Or make your own ice cream sundae parties. Or heck, we could just go out on the National Mall and ride bikes. Wait there for the ice cream truck.

Anything but try to act like grownups.

61

When Good Teams Produce Bad Results

Let's make an agreement: You and I will go along with the team.

And if the product is less than optimal, at least we got along.

If the requirements make no sense because the client thinks he knows marketing better than we do, we'll deal with it.

If the project scope bleeds until its outer limits are unrecognizable, we'll cope.

If the timeline gets drastically shortened while you were out of the office for a tooth cleaning, no problem.

If the demands are much more than we can actually deliver — whatever you do, don't kick up a fuss. At least not now.

If the logo and tagline are completely off the mark, but they've been approved up and down the chain, with no hassle — please lay off with the criticism.

Don't mess up the flow of the team. It depends on all of us getting along.

It's important that you understand that.

If you do the best you can, and I do the best I can, and none of us make any waves, ever — well then there isn't much more one could ask for.

Is there?

62

A Simpler Way to Manage People

A few years ago I had an interview for a supervisory job at an agency that shall remain nameless.

"What would you do with a workforce that is largely unmotivated?" the interviewer asked me. "How would you get them going again?"

On that day I must have been unmotivated, too.

"I don't know," I said. "I can't make miracles."

Needless to say, I did not get the job. But I've heard that question, or a variation of it, in nearly every single senior-level interview I've been on.

In the beginning I thought the right answer was to have an answer. Now I know that the way to handle this one is to talk about an approach, a process. Preferably an integrated one that handles people in a consistent way, from beginning to end.

It is unfortunate that the federal government is not set up to manage its human resources very well right now. Even the most qualified people find gaining entry difficult. Leaders say the right things, but their actions disappoint. Middle managers are routinely stressed out, compressed as they are between the demands of supervising work and having to do it themselves.

Performance management is both a battlefield and a minefield, and it takes up so much time the incentive is more to minimize pain than to maximize productivity. And an overwhelming aversion to risk, change or newness tends to alienate the very people who can serve as a source of transformation.

I didn't go into the government looking to be a human capital expert, but life here has taken me down that path, because that's precisely what you do when you focus on internal communications, help supervisors document performance management issues, or become a supervisor yourself. All of these are experiences I've had in the government, and they have frequently been painful because the system itself is broken.

Branding people don't often talk about this, but they do a fair amount of human capital work as well. People who don't believe in the organization's vision, mission, values or desired image are not going to do very much to support it. This means they'll either fight with each other, create stovepipes, disengage, or leave the organization altogether — frequently taking their top-flight talents with them.

So I've ended up immersed in this world of strategic human capital management. Reviewing Federal Employee Viewpoint Survey results for articles about results and trends. Participating in the interagency Federal Communicators Network and events, which frequently lead to conversations about how we manage our people and how we could do it better.

On every occasion, joining others who asked a similar

question: How can we make things better?

As a branding person and a human being with a lot on her plate, I long ago came to agree with simplicity experts Alan Siegel and Irene Etzkorn that reducing complexity is the answer. As the former co-chair of the Federal Communicators Network, Dave Hebert puts it, "In the perfect world, HR would be completely plugged in. You connect with people virtually, identify an opportunity for them to contribute, and make it happen, without a lot of paperwork."

Simplicity, accessibility, relevant information delivered conveniently — this is the plea I hear from colleagues governmentwide, again and again, especially when it comes to onboarding. Bridget Roddy and I have worked together several times to bring students into agencies through the State Department's Virtual Student Foreign Service, a gateway to public service through which 16 federal agencies permit college students to work remotely.

Bridget believes that technology would go a long way toward providing an answer. "The civic graph concept can connect everyone who wants to be a part of public service, or is already there," she says. "We ought to have a Facebook-like connective tissue for government."

I met Lisa Nelson toward the end of last year, in her capacity as leader of the GSA's Open Opportunities program. She helped me figure out how to use the program, a rapidly growing professional development initiative that allows federal employees to "moonlight" at other agencies, gaining skills and establishing a broad network of peers they can turn to when they have questions or immediate problems to solve. Open Opportunities develops and connects the federal workforce deploying skills and expertise across the government when and where they are needed.

A longtime government employee, Lisa believes that success lies in finding talent buried in agency silos. And so while she thinks an integrated approach to managing human capital is a noble goal, she believes we must build a network of innovators, passionate, mission-driven individuals who can make a bigger impact if they are connected to other like-minded federal workers. To that end, "we must promote a cooperative approach to problem-solving," says Lisa. "This will help agencies and employees gain skills, talent and interagency experience."

The Partnership for Public Service recently held its annual awards ceremony, where Bridget was a finalist for the Call to Service medal. "Cross-agency collaboration is everything," she told me. "It was all they talked about all night." Which is all well and good, I wondered, but who would be in charge if we created an all-encompassing, interagency "HR Central?" Even beyond the "Collaboration Central" envisioned by GSA?

None of my colleagues had the answer for this. Start a new post inside the White House? Restructure the Office of Personnel Management? Form a working group with a representative inside every federal agency?

Having raised two millennials, one thing is for certain: Tomorrow's federal employees won't have the patience for us to figure this out.

63

20 Lessons Learned From Great Federal Government Managers

Show you are a valuable asset by being selfless and helpful. That's lesson 1.

Here are the rest:

1. Travel with a posse. It makes you look important.
2. Delegate. Repeat that a hundred times.
3. Help people – give them credit – promote them – and maintain good relationships for life.
4. Ask for help. This is not the same as delegating. Find resources.
5. Overcommunicate, and collaborate genuinely.
6. Work around red tape. Do not fight it.
7. Be quietly effective most of the time, but know when to be loud.
8. Don't make enemies if you can help it.
9. Be nice to everyone, no matter what.
10. Don't take it personally.
11. Understand when something is a lost cause. Walk away.

12. Remember what's really important and go home on time.
13. Also remember it's all a game.
14. Be passionate about excellence. That's not just a line.
15. Have a clear competitor in mind. This is not the same thing as an enemy.
16. Learn one skill from everyone you meet.
17. Understand how truly ignorant you are.
18. Stay out of things that are not your business.
19. Be humble and grateful, but don't pass up a chance to shine.

XIII

Personal Life

64

10 Tips for Federal Employees on the Personal Use Of Social Media

Years ago the Federal Communicators Network Professional Standards Working Group released social media tips for federal employees. I was part of the steering committee and a volunteer in this effort to promote the development of governmentwide standards for professional conduct and quality communication.

Notes and Disclaimers

- The tips below are meant to help clarify some issues that federal employees may not be aware of, or that may be confusing.
- The list is not meant to replace a thorough review of law, policy, and official guidance or to restrict or alter federal employees' rights and responsibilities in any way.
- When in doubt, please do not use this as a substitute for obtaining reliable direction from an official source. If you work for a federal agency, there may be specific guidance

that pertains to you.
- Like all FCN documents, this is unofficial in nature.
- Volunteers' opinions, as well as publications, do not represent official guidance, the views of their federal agencies, or the views of the government as a whole.

These tips may be freely reproduced and distributed. If you do so, please include the disclaimer above so that readers are not misled into thinking that this is an official government document.

The 10 Tips

1. First Amendment Rights: **Your personal social media profiles are your own**, and for the most part, the federal government does not intend to control online activities that are purely personal (an example of an exception is the Hatch Act, which contains certain limits on employee free speech). Also, the same principles apply whether your speech occurs over social media or in more traditional ways, e.g. publishing a letter to the editor of a newspaper.

2. Special Restrictions: **Find out from your agency whether there are any special restrictions on your social media activity** beyond the general rules that apply to all federal employees. For example, this might apply if you work for a law enforcement agency.

3. If You Are Aware of Misconduct: **Reporting fraud, waste and abuse to the appropriate authorities is lawful, but leaking classified or otherwise confidential information over the internet is not**.

4. Disclaimer: When people know that you work for the government, they are prone to assuming that you speak for the government, even when you're not. So in discussing your personal views, it helps to **be upfront about the fact that you are not speaking in an official capacity**. Example: "The content of this communication is entirely my own and does not reflect the opinions of or endorsement by any federal agency or the government as a whole."

5. Opinions about Your Agency: **You are entitled to discuss, analyze or disagree with your agency about publicly available information. That said, your agency may require you to tell them** if you do so. Check your public affairs/public communications policy for more information, and do not hesitate to ask your Office of Public Affairs and/or your ethics officer for guidance.

6. No "Impersonation": While you are free to describe your interests, experiences and ideas on unofficial time, **do not use unofficial time or personal social media accounts to act as an official representative of your agency without authorization**.

7. Political Activity: Regarding personal political activity, **read the Hatch Act**. (The text is readily available online, along with an extensive set of frequently asked questions.)

8. No Right to Privacy on Work Devices: Read and follow your agency's policies on information technology use. Some allow you to use your work computer to access your personal accounts on a limited basis. If you do use your work device, whether desktop computer or mobile phone, to access personal accounts, understand that

your activity may be monitored by the agency.

9. Keep Personal Devices Personal: **Don't use your personal devices or accounts for agency activity**, because then it is subject to legal discovery (including FOIA) in the event of litigation. Also, use "smart" passwords (guidance on these is readily available online), and change them frequently.

10. Targeting by Foreign Spies: **Be careful who you "friend" online**. Foreign intelligence agents are known to target federal employees specifically, for a variety of reasons.

5 Additional Suggestions:

1. You are allowed to be a human being. Human beings have lives, have experiences, move through the world, and experience things. We have opinions and we disagree. You do not have to be afraid to be human and also be online. You just have to be mindful of what you are doing, and who is watching, as any reasonable person would.

2. Generalize experiences and do not refer to specific instances or individuals. It's fine to say that meetings are boring for example. But do not refer to that specific gathering on that specific day at that specific time in that specific room with that specific department. Led by that specific person. Similarly, don't discuss the specifics of your day-to-day work. I know it is possible for the agency to be comfortable with this. I personally do not think it's a good idea. To my mind, it interferes with operations. Similarly, don't try to explain the agency's policies, programs or procedures; don't take a position on what the agency does or does not do. Again, you

run the risk of interfering with operations and you also might share information that is not already public.

3. When you say what you think or feel, it's fine to be honest, but it's important to be respectful too. You hold a position of public trust. Ask yourself, if someone took these words and printed them in the newspaper, would most people question my ability to serve?

4. Humor is great but something to be handled with kid gloves. You do not want to seem hateful, attacking, divisive, racist, sexist, and so on (hopefully you are not these things, either). It is the nature of a joke that it will often be politically incorrect. That's why jokes, especially politically incorrect jokes, are often a bad idea. This doesn't mean you have to be "heavy" all the time. It is OK to be yourself, to lighten up every now and then. Just understand the potential impact of your words.

5. Focus on objectively advancing knowledge, best practice, community. Look for points of commonality. Try to reach across the boundaries of government, private sector, academia. There are many controversies, many issues to be hashed out, and you can contribute to all these discussions. Federal employees are generally extremely well-educated and articulate. This is where we shine.

65

How to Comment on Social Media

Commenting and writing are really two different things. There are many books, articles, presentations and 1-2-3 posts that will tell you how to build a professional presence online. The general idea is to build a body of work that proves to the world you are a credible, trustworthy presence in whatever sphere you claim to operate in.

While commenting is a form of writing, the emphasis is different. After all, comments are a reaction, they are inherently defensive, whereas the act of putting something out there is proactive and creative. So you need to have good reason for saying what you say.

We are living in defensive times. Every word you put out there matters. It establishes who you are. Your opinions will be scrutinized; your command of the facts, and how you articulate them, portrays you as either a respectable person or a fake, flake or dummy.

No matter how benign your words, somebody out there will at some point take offense. You may deserve a challenge or a correction on legitimate grounds. Or, they may get ideological with you. They may attack you personally. You comment, they comment and suddenly it is an endless and unproductive protracted debate that makes everyone look bad.

So what are the qualities that make social media comments most effective? What are the things you should avoid? Here are some dos and don'ts to keep in mind:

Do:

- Identify yourself if you can.
- Say what you have to say without censoring yourself.
- Express your truly held beliefs.
- Share facts that can be independently validated, or opinion columns with the caveat that this line of thinking makes sense to you or is a good read (but obviously you are not expected to validate it).
- Refer people to a source where they can independently assess the quality of the information you're providing.
- Be polite and respectful, remembering that you are talking to an actual person.
- Hold people accountable for the implications of what they are saying, but recognize common ground first, if you can.
- Generally, help to further a productive dialogue that gets people closer to the essence of whatever topic is under discussion.
- Make statements of support for what another person is going through or sharing of an emotional nature.

Don't:

- Censor yourself because you are afraid other people won't like you.

- Behave recklessly. You've heard the term *drunk tweeting*? Don't let that be you.
- Say things that you know have no basis in fact.
- Attack people for having a certain opinion.
- Engage in personal attacks or make offensive statements.
- Make reckless statements.
- Take money in exchange for making comments that appear to be un-sponsored. It's one thing to announce yourself, but quite another to lie.
- Tell people that they have no right to post a certain thing on a certain platform because there are other places that are more appropriate—you are not the platform police.

XIV

Politicals

66

How to Serve a President You Don't Like

By default in every administration, some federal employees will be "yuge" proponents of the winning candidate, and others will truly dislike the person. They may even think the president is the worst thing ever to happen to the country and does not deserve to be in office.

But you do not have to like the president to serve well, to make your agency more functional, and to deliver great service to the American public. When President Obama took office in 2009, it was a very happy moment for me as a citizen, at the time. But even when my feelings changed—and over time they did change sharply—I was still able to serve, and serve well. Because whatever program I was working on, it had little or nothing to do with the president and everything to do with the citizen. The more effectively and efficiently I contributed, and helped others to contribute, the better we served the taxpayers, who too often are forgotten in all the discord.

Many conflicts in government really are about ideological

differences and beliefs that are fervently held. Others are about personality differences. Still others have to do with money, status, and power. Many are a mixture of all of these.

But most federal employees aren't having these power struggles. Quite honestly, they're just getting by, maybe trying to learn something along the way, trying to contribute what they can. They want to take care of themselves and their kids; they want to hang out with their friends and live normally in what feels like an increasingly unstable world.

Most civil servants, at least, can serve a president they don't like. But if doing you job under this president means violating your personal beliefs and principles, then I would argue it's incumbent upon you to find another place to work outside of government. To me, there is a seditious quality to remaining in government while working covertly to thwart the administration.

But even if you do not like President Trump and you do not agree with his policies or his approach to things, you can function well if you focus on the taxpayers. Ask yourself:

- What can you do to explain what's going on, respond to questions, make it easier to access information and services taxpayers are entitled to, and decipher the byzantine ways of the government?
- What can you do to make it easier to work with your agency?
- What can you do to increase your agency's accountability, its adherence to process and its mission?
- Who can you partner with in other agencies to do a better job? Look for free resources for leadership training; track down the experts in subjects you need to know about.

Find out how you can access technology support without having to use a vendor.

- What kind of social media campaigns can you build to educate the public about the benefits your agency brings to local communities and nationwide?
- What can you do to make your agency's data available so private citizens, researchers and business can access it and use it?
- How can you help the media provide accurate information about your agency and its mission?
- How can you rebrand valuable programs that may have been championed by a prior administration, and are therefore overlooked or minimized today? Perhaps you can reach out and educate new appointees about the importance of the work and the opportunity for them to leverage it as a pillar of their own success.

Let's be a little entrepreneurial here. Times change. Even if you do not like the current administration, you may serve a president you like better at some point down the road (or you may find the next one is someone you love to hate even more). The point is, the civil service isn't about liking or disliking any one leader. It's about the effective, disinterested oversight and management of the organizations that deliver critical services to citizens. If you work in government, you have an opportunity to make things better.

XV

Project Management

67

Why Everyone Should Master Project Management Skills

Agile, waterfall, MS Project, Excel, or even a plain old Sharpie—you somehow have to manage your work. And most of what we do in our daily lives, if we are in a professional setting, involves a series of projects.

Project management is boring. I know you're telling yourself that, and you think that, and other people tell you that too. "I am a certified project manager" just does not have anywhere near the appeal of something like, "I am the chief marketing officer at YazDeboo" (whatever YazDeboo is, they must make something cool) or "I am a rocket scientist at NASA."

I get that. But if you're doing project management right it is not boring at all because the art and the science of it is to simultaneously juggle a lot of different mini-initiatives aimed at specific outcomes, while ultimately shoring up your reputation, which is the value you bring to the table.

The outcome of a project affects your brand:

- How you implement a customer relationship management (CRM) platform, for example, leads your customers to view you in a very particular way.
- Hiring someone is another project. Maybe you didn't think of it that way, but it is. The kind of people you hire and the manner in which you onboard them will ultimately affect your organization's character, and character manifests itself in the values stakeholders see in everyday behaviors.
- Designing or redesigning your organizational chart is another project (and whoa, this can be a bear to undertake). But the manner in which you categorize and stovepipe your institutional structures (and all structures must be put into buckets, even if they're very broad) will affect the way you define the work you're doing. Just to give a very basic example, if you put Digital Communications into the IT shop, the output will be vastly different than if IT serves Digital Communications.

Outcomes are shaped by the way you conduct your projects. Your processes either reinforce your company's ability to function as a unified whole (e.g., a recognizable brand with a recognizable vision, mission, culture and values) or they are crisis-driven, dysfunctional and corrosive.

If you incorporate the principles of project management into your projects large and small— following a work breakdown structure, keeping to a schedule, accepting and modulating stakeholder feedback—you create a safe and stable space within which employees trust that they can do their best work. You're not in crisis mode, and as such, you can grow and flourish without constantly looking over your shoulder.

If you ignore irresponsible, abusive, or corrupt behavior by senior leaders, and ignore the warning signs of trouble, at some point disaster will occur. That disaster will create a cleanup project (or many cleanup projects). And you will naturally attract employees who don't really care about doing things well, but only about covering for messes and looking valuable as they do it. In fact one could say that such employees will actually enable future conflicts, avoiding the unpleasant task of providing negative feedback and instead positioning themselves as "fixers."

Contrary to what most people think, branding is not about ad campaigns and logos. Those are dessert. Your main meal is the unglamorous work you do to keep things functioning every day.

I once worked for a boss who was famous. When I complained about having to do so many dreary things she said to me, "Only a tiny percentage of life is fun. The rest is just horse manure. Roll up your sleeves—plenty of that to go around."

XVI

Public Affairs

68

The Most Hated Job In Government

In an uncharacteristically direct comment, my friend asked, somewhat rhetorically: "The government does not need PR people at all, do they?"

"What do you mean by that?" I replied.

"Just give out the information," said my friend. "Don't pay people to lie."

It's a common perception that civil servants are lazy, overpaid and incompetent. And when it comes to government public affairs specialists, there is an accompanying stereotype: We're not only lazy, overpaid and incompetent, but also a gang of bought-and-paid-for, lying propagandists. Since PR has such a sleazy reputation, it's inevitable that people don't like PR people very much, and the anger is magnified on social media:

- "Shill" is the term used to describe an individual, paid or sponsored, who solely represents one side of an issue.
- "Astroturfing" is the practice of misrepresenting marketing messages to make them appear as grassroots

support—generating fake buzz.
- "Trolling" is the art of deliberately provoking people online who are just expressing their opinion.

Let us be clear: The government should not be paying shills, astroturfers or trolls. It is, in fact, illegal for the government to spend appropriated dollars (i.e. tax money) to propagandize. But public relations, properly done, is not about lying.

The job of a public relations (what we in government call "public affairs") specialist is to translate official activity such that the public can understand it. The difference between providing information and providing translation is that you are explaining what's going on in terms that the public can understand.

Unfortunately, over the course of many decades, government public relations specialists have been used, abused, and kicked around. As a result, the integrity of government communicators is constantly questioned. When they're only transmitting what has already been approved by others in the agency. The U.S. government is fortunate to have many laws, policies and standards that apply to official communication. But that framework is only as good as its enforcement.

If you're hating on government public relations specialists, your anger is misdirected.

Always look at the system. Never at a single person.

69

Spending On Government Communications Is Ripe for Abuse

Last year the Government Accountability Office issued "Public Relations Spending" (GAO-16-877R) in response to a request from the Senate Budget Committee. The purpose of the report was to "determine how much the federal government spends on public relations activities, including contracts and internal agency support, and identify the highest-spending agencies."

"Public relations internal agency support" is defined in the report as employees classified as "public affairs specialists" (GS-1035s). Right away we have a contradiction in terms, because a public affairs specialist, as opposed to a PR professional, gives you data, not "spin." The report offers this definition of a public affairs specialist:

> "*Public Affairs occupational series are responsible for administering, supervising, or performing work involved in establishing and maintaining communication between federal agencies and the public. Among other things, their work includes identifying communi-*

cation needs and developing informational materials
on agency policies, programs, services, and activities."

The GAO categorizes legitimate communication activity as follows:

- Public education and awareness
- Customer service
- General information and recruitment
- Compliance with laws and policies

If they do nothing else, the government's communicators can and should explain to the 325 million people who live in the United States what exactly the government did with the $3.9 trillion it spent in 2016. (To that end, check out this very neat infographic from the Congressional Budget Office.)

It is not clear how many communicators the government has on hand. In 2014, the federal government employed 5,086 public affairs specialists, representing .28 percent of all federal employees; 42 percent of them worked for the Department of Defense. (The GAO report only counted these employees.)

However, agencies employ many other communicators, including agency leadership, "writer–editors," information technology specialists (web content), management & program analysts, "unclassified" personnel, and others, such as policy and technical subject matter experts.

It is also not clear how much the government is spending on contract personnel engaged in public affairs work. The GAO report notes that "federal obligations for advertising and public relations contracts have, on average, been close to $1 billion annually over the past decade."

With regard to reporting on contract spending, data quality is limited. GAO notes that these contracts "do not capture the full scope of these activities" because it is possible to issue relevant contracts under other categories.

Also, I am not aware of any database that specifically distinguishes between federal contract spending on personnel (e.g. a graphic designer), and on services (e.g. a billboard).

Finally, the GAO definition of "advertising/public relations" intermingles legitimate and questionable spending, e.g. "communication," "image-building," "to inform or persuade."

Poor evaluative data quality (note: not the quality of government data) is the main reason reason why government messaging sucks, and the government has the lowest public trust scores ever, despite all the good work being done and despite all the money being thrown at doing it. For both internal control and accountability purposes, you've got to clearly identify what you're trying to do, what the reason is, and how much you spent on each relevant aspect of the effort. And then ask an impartial third party, how well did that work?

Here is an example of a known best practice: the annual plain language "report card" scores agencies receive. Here's another: the ongoing Web analytics agencies collect. But there's a limitation, though: Are we talking about the right things in the first place? Could some, or much of our content be collapsed and integrated, to make it easier and more useful for the public to access?

Which brings up another conversation we should have: whether communication should be defined as inherently governmental work. I believe it is, for the most part: the basic definition is work "so intimately related to the public interest as to require performance by Federal Government employees."

The reality is that the federal communicator must, to do a good job, be knowledgeable about the agency's operations and culture, and be dedicated to the mission. As well, they typically also have invaluable institutional knowledge and commitment and a familiarity with stakeholders that cannot be easily duplicated. This is a federal communicator's brand.

A contractor's primary focus, as it should be, is the amount of money they can make.

The fact that most federal communication is outsourced, in my view, makes us vulnerable to the shortcomings of all commodity products. What agencies need are critically thinking personnel. The contracting relationship simply does not provide for that. And money wasted on expensive, ill-conceived projects (the client's fault, not the contractor's) contributes to the negative perception that government communication is money wasted on fluff.

I do believe contractors can be helpful, particularly where technical knowledge is lacking. But the government relies on them far too much. As an alternative, interagency consulting is a promising area for the government to explore. When you bring in a third party from within the government to assist, you get the benefit of expertise and an objective point of view.

The bottom line is this: To do a good job at something, you have to be able to measure it. Then set goals, and then determine where your work is coming up short. Right now, we aren't measuring, and we aren't counting or measuring a dedicated communication staff or chain of command—within or across agencies. The function is not managed as a unified whole.

As such, communication spending is ripe for waste and abuse.

70

Civil Servants Need to Stay Out of the Spin Business

The fact that government communications is ripe for abuse has undoubtedly contributed to trust levels in government that are at their lowest ever. While political corruption is chiefly responsible for public disillusionment (e.g. "Vietnam: The Loss Of American Innocence?") it is also true that outsized spending on federal public relations contracts, as well as propagandistic agency communications play a role. Though the Government Accountability Office has long recognized that appropriately used communication is one of the government's top five internal controls, the way in which federal communications has been abused is not just wrong, but has also turned its dedicated practitioners into a public joke.

Fortunately, there are a number of efforts underway to remedy this situation. In the U.S. military, the nature and scope of the public affairs function has been codified. In the U.K., civil service communicators now have clear guidance as well. In the U.S., federal agencies and employees, including the Federal Communicators Network of which I am a part, are working to update and implement proper standards and prevent manipulation of statutory requirements that prohibit self-promotion and propaganda.

To give just one example, the General Services Administration has developed a short list of questions to be considered before requirements are written for advertising and marketing contracts. (Considering that we are talking about hundreds of millions of dollars, this is not a small advance.) These questions force the person writing the requirements to consider not only whether the proposed contract will violate the law, but also this crucial question: "Is the statement of work so broadly written that it could be interpreted to condone or encourage any of the activities described above? If the answer is yes, the statement of work/Request for Quotations is not yet ready for issuance."

It is easy to be pessimistic about government; as citizens we are regularly cautioned not to trust it. As former British ambassador Craig Murray, who lost his job for speaking out about human rights abuses, once put it: "As a rule of thumb, if the government wants you to know it, it probably isn't true."

You can argue, as well, that a healthy distrust of government is not just good, but patriotic; with that I tend to agree.

But it is also true that we should not rest our laurels on the inevitability of alienation.

The fact is that we do have a country, a country needs a government, and as civil servants in particular we have a responsibility to help see to it that the government functions well.

71

Don't Let Your Message Morph Into Propaganda

I have worked for the federal government since 2003 across half a dozen agencies and not once has anyone ever instructed me to lie. Not once.

But there are many ways to lie. What used to be merely disingenuous on the government's part—a way to avoid controversy, maintain credibility, and try to look good—can be downright dangerous.

In just a few short years, all of us have developed an incredibly sophisticated vocabulary when it comes to decoding the signals and symbols of communication.

In the past, we woke up in the morning and we read the newspaper on the train. Some of us watched the morning news or listened to the news highlights on the radio, driving to work or school.

Not so much today.

The ubiquity and power of social media means that people consume information continuously. Where there used to be an absolute Berlin Wall between fact and opinion, the lines have blurred. As the presidential election made absolutely clear, that reliable construct has clearly fallen.

Branding has been with us for many, many years, too. It is of course the construction of a common fantasy, and for the dream you pay a very specific price premium.

But in the past I think we all knew, or at least had a certain respect for, the belief that there are some things which are "image" and some that are real. For example, President John F. Kennedy had many mistresses while maintaining the image of a marriage. But as a President we admired him, and still do, for his very real humanity, patriotism and vision.

Today branding proliferates to such a crazy extent that we ourselves sometimes forget when we're "being the personal brand" and when we're being real.

It is against this backdrop of a blurry, propagandistic information landscape that the President enters with his or her agenda and political appointees. They must explain their policies to the public, and they must also provide data that the public can rely on.

In essence, this is a contradictory mission. For it will inevitably occur that data contradicts the message.

While of course there are many safeguards built in to prevent the politicization of the civil service, the mental block persists among "civils" and "politicals" against sharing information that "will make the government look bad."

As we say in D.C., "you don't want to find yourself on the cover of the *Washington Post.*"

Often this means that it takes agencies a long time to respond to issues, get data out unless they feel it's totally impossible to misinterpret, or simply just to enter into dialogue with dogged critics.

All of this is a terrible mistake and leads to the politicization of what should be a very vanilla, neutral repository for information that everyone trusts, regardless of their political persuasion.

We should re-examine the communication function within government, and establish a cadre of professionals who operate according to recognized standards independent of whatever agency they serve. Their work should be evaluated every year against published standards, not for "return on investment" but for the extent to which it is factually accurate and is trusted by the public, not government officials.

72

How to Field Questions From the Public Like a Pro

No matter where you work, you will at some point have to answer questions from the public. It might be an employee, a journalist, a customer, or even a member of Congress.

Now this may sound obvious, but most of the time people have better things to do than sit down and contact you with their concerns. So if they're exercised enough to do that, there is probably something significant on their minds.

And while you may think it's easy to simply respond, here are a few tips that may help you build your reputation for integrity by handling public inquiries effectively.

Mechanics: Acknowledge the inquiry. Give the question a ticket number. Answer within a reasonable period of time. Make it clear when they should expect to hear from you.

Basic Content: Get to the point immediately. Make sure you answer all the questions or address all the issues raised. Keep responses short and provide links to further information. Don't answer more than was originally asked.

Scope: Be thorough. Go the extra mile to offer alternatives, options and resources. However, don't speculate about things you don't know or can't back up.

Attitude: Talk like a grownup talking to a grownup. Don't be condescending or robotic. Be respectful. Be compassionate. Explain your reasoning or the basis for what you're saying. Take responsibility as appropriate—some complaints will have nothing to do with you.

No-Nos: Do not ask your technical experts to write. Check for spelling errors. Even a minor error makes you look unprofessional, careless and untrustworthy.

Here's the most important thing to remember: Be present. Focus on this person, this inquiry, this moment in time.

Think about how they will feel when they read your response. Imagine that you botch it and infuriate the recipient, escalating the problem.

Or, the opposite—they are surprised and delighted by the personalized, professional, comprehensive answer they received from you. They appreciate of your humanity, your intelligence, and most of all your accountability.

73

How Messaging Can Suck the Life Out of Your Agency's Brand

When I first started working for the government in 2003, I noticed that the employees around me had many different versions of "the truth."

I noticed that many were bitter. That they frequently greeted new ideas with "we've done all this before, and then some."

Some of my colleagues were downright resigned. They just didn't care. They had "checked out," and virtually nothing was going to bring them back save some really good news about their TSP.

I remember that I was hired because of my brand expertise, but that the view of branding at that time was very much tied to pretty pictures.

Quickly I learned that the higher you went in the organization, the more forward-thinking the leaders, and also the more realistic they were about what could and could not be done.

Executives really did say all the things they should have

been saying. Their minds were in the right place, and I can say this with confidence because I regularly had the good fortune to be in the presence of heads of agencies. Even, rarely, to interview them.

But where things began to break down was in the "how" of executive communication. Because you really had to be in the presence of senior leadership to understand what the agency was doing and why.

Not to engage in hyperbole, but it seemed to me there was way too much overthinking of every word everybody said "officially." The words "written by committee" don't even begin to cover it.

There was a hypersensitivity to the what-ifs of this phrasing, that phrasing, the other thing.

To the point where in the end, executive messages really said nothing at all.

I am not arguing for a particular policy about communication here. It's really about theory: a higher level of strategic thinking is due.

When we consider how unmotivated and angry our employees are, the first order of business ought to be how to get them back in the ring. Engaging in, at the very least, the act of reading what executives are saying.

I don't think people should be speaking out of turn, paraphrasing or making up the messaging in their heads.

I do think there should be far more movement inside the government toward encouraging employees at the highest levels, designated speakers, to speak freely and frankly, on as many occasions at possible.

I think communicators ought to pull back, other than helping senior leaders to think through what they want to say, as needed.

There may be fears that words will be misinterpreted. They will be.

But at the end of the day, the damaged morale and rampant mistrust that comes from vanilla, puttylike "official words" is far worse than normal human awkwardness. And the occasional gaffe.

Employees, and the public, can forgive a lot of things.

It's when they don't care anymore that the government has a real problem.

74

The Difference Between Public Affairs and Public Relations

On the positive side, federal communicators are extraordinarily sharp people (and have always been). Also positive, the sophistication level in terms of technique and in terms of the demand for transparency is growing by leaps and bounds. Just in the past five years, it's literally amazing to me.

Furthermore positive, I have always known agency leaders to be sophisticated in terms of their ability to read the tea leaves and to exercise good judgment. One memory in particular stands out of Robert Bonner, the former head of U.S. Customs and Border Protection. Bonner was amazing — he used to scribble out *all* of my drafts of his executive message for the monthly magazine and write it himself. I remember that handwriting!

But there is a less positive side that hopefully we will overcome. And that is the failure to distinguish in theoretical terms between "public affairs" and "public relations." Many times, more times than I can count, I have personally experienced frustration that agencies were not as forthcoming as they could be because there was a prevailing opinion that silence is golden.

This is not tied to one administration or another, rather it's a constant battle between those who generally want to "avoid trouble," and in their shortsighted view this means not talking about problems for fear of provoking (insert exaggerated worry).

Unfortunately I've seen communicators suffer because they were perceived as too open, because they did not understand the unwritten rules.

What is really sad, to me, is the contradiction between the incredible integrity of public servants and the incredible distrust the public has for the government. And every single time we open up and are transparent, we find ourselves rewarded with greater trust — just the opposite of what is feared.

Where things do go wrong — and of course they do — the best course of action is to tell it early, tell it often, tell it clearly, and be overall matter-of-fact about it. This is not just good government practice it's good PR practice as well.

At the end of the day, the key difference between private sector PR and government public affairs is who is paying the bill and what expectations they're bound by. The private sector PR expert is trying to help their client resuscitate or enhance their image. The government public affairs expert is trying to help the taxpayer get the information they need and, more broadly, trying to help the government function effectively and efficiently.

Confusion over this distinction is the source of another hornet's nest of misunderstanding, and that is the term "branding." The word means "propaganda" to so many, but for government it actually means doing a better job at communication — unifying the agency inside and giving the public a consistent and useful experience on the outside.

75

Colliding With The Third Rail

It is the classic dilemma of a corporate mouthpiece: the client doesn't want to talk.

- Crisis? "Let's wait for the lawyers."
- Bad news? "It'll blow over."
- Gossip? "Just ignore that."

The underlying assumption is always the same, too: "If you give them any attention, you're only legitimizing their argument."

Recently I learned this term, "the third rail." As in supersensitive, controversial topics too dangerous for a politician to discuss.

Whether you're in politics or not, it is unfailingly "third rail" for a communicator to argue with the client's discomfort at arguing their case in the court of public opinion.

One of the all-time best theorists of organizational dysfunction, Chris Argyris, called the failure to question assumptions a problem of "double-loop learning." That is to say, unhealthy organizations not only take certain incorrect things for granted, but they resist — almost to the death, and sometimes fatally — any attempt to critically examine those beliefs.

In an unhealthy organization, communication about things that matter is impossible, because:

- Problems are denied until they become an unpleasant crisis. The prevalent belief: "out of sight, out of mind."
- Crises are ignored until they become catastrophes: "Talking about problems only makes them real."
- Great communicators, who recognize what's going on and try to moderate the effect by opening the spigot of speech, are viewed as a threat and eliminated.

A very long time ago I printed a thousand pages of research on a very real crisis that was about to explode, and did explode, and it was awful.

But this was before it happened. And the person to whom I showed it looked at the pile of paper and turned to me and said: "Be careful."

The person who said this was not my "enemy." Just the opposite – they were obviously concerned for my professional welfare.

Because I'd hit that third rail, full-on, dead center. If I pressed forward any further, I'd undoubtedly cross the red-hot, nuclear "red line."

In the end I let it go. I had reached the limits of my effectiveness and my pay grade; persistence would only have served to get me fired.

In the many years since I've come close to that "third

rail" many a time. And I think I've figured out the secret to putting your hand on that molten iron, without coming away irretrievably burned.

You realize this: Bad situations build up over time. They're complex; they're multi-stakeholder; they normally involve a really smelly stew of greed, sometimes sex, and the lust for power. Only the fool would dare to step in without knowing if they're pulling on the red wire that sets off the bomb, or the green one that defuses it.

Most errors in judgment involve ignorance like this, plus a healthy measure of ego – wanting to be the best, to solve the intractable problem that seemingly nobody else could get their arms around.

A better course of action, if you're a communicator? Look around you, keep your instinctive and emotional antennae high, speak calmly and logically about what you see, talk about risk, but most importantly, draw in "the wisdom of the team."

By working together, leveraging the power of multiple intelligences, knowledge bases and institutional memories — plus the innate desire we all have to make a difference — the chances of succeeding are much greater than they are when you go it alone.

Even if you can't make a dent in this round, you're more likely to live to fight another day.

76

Intelligent PR Is Never Propaganda

Communicators spend a lot of time working on getting the message right. To an extent that is a good thing. For in the day-to-day of organizational life, the message can sometimes get lost in the weeds. It is important to align and focus everyone, from leaders on down, on communicating what matters most.

When it comes to the brand, there is nothing more important than communication. "Build it and they will come" is bogus. You've got to say the right thing, at the right time, just to build buzz. And then protect your buzz from a blooper caught on Facebook that can bring you down. Caution is natural, necessary and appropriate.

But despite all this, regardless of the benefits of coordinated messaging, most brands don't know how to use a brand playbook well. They either follow it too religiously ("Have I provided you excellent customer service today?"); implement it incorrectly ("Qwikster"); or ignore it altogether and just make things up as they go along (Sears).

Branding is confusing to a lot of people. But when it comes

to brand communication, only one rule, if broken, can destroy you: Never, never peddle propaganda.

77

Keep It Ego-Free

Marketing is not an easy profession. It is actually pretty freaking hard.

The job of a marketer is to persuade people that they need something. Or someone. And then sell it to them.

How easy is it to...

Get a 4-year-old to eat carrots?

Get into Harvard?

Get a job?

Get married?

Get someone elected?

Get someone to literally buy whatever it is that you sell?

All of these things involve marketing. And if they were so easy, we would all be rich, happy and retired.

Yet the most popular misconception about marketing – after the belief that we are all a bunch of liars – is the idea that it is "all about the message."

Meaning that if you can only find the exact right thing to say, your audience will believe you.

As if people are so stupid.

Believing that marketing is "messaging" is really just a form of ego massage.

"I am wonderful, here are the reasons, now I've succeeded in marketing to you."

A better way to think of marketing is like listening actively and then responding.

"How are you? Tell me about it."

And then when the customer has told you, and told you, and told you...you validate what they've said.

"I hear that. You feel —. You want —. Let me see what I can do about that."

And then you do it.

While it is true that people often can't articulate what they want, it is also true that they don't want you to "message" them.

Marketing is listening. It is ego-free.

If you do it properly, the audience pays you to listen.

If you do it the wrong way, you are talking and talking and their minds are a million miles away.

78

5 Ways To Work Effectively With The Media: Tips For Federal Communicators

Often I hear people ask about how to work with the media more effectively. They worry about reporters who "just don't seem to like us," who "give us a hard time about everything," and so on.

The assumption behind this question is that reporters are somehow "out to get" their sources. Not a helpful place to begin, because it presupposes a negative outcome from the start.

Here are some things I've learned over time from personal experience working with reporters, talking to them, and from observing the experiences of others.

1. Reporters are motivated by public service, just like federal workers. It's a thankless job. They go into it because they care. Have the same respect for them that you want them to have for you.

2. Reporters want to speak with sources directly. Don't speak on their behalf, don't translate, don't be the intermediary, just arrange for the interview.

3. Reporters find it hard to gain access to good sources. Your value as a public affairs officer lies in your connecting the reporter with the high-value source. Even better, combine the source with high-value open data that is easy to find on your website.

4. Reporters don't instinctively understand your subject matter. You may think that your agency's mission, operations, policies and procedures are intuitive, but they're normally extremely hard to understand for outsiders. Make it simple for them to understand. This is different from high-value sources and open data, because the value lies in simplification rather than the availability of complicated, primary sources

5. Reporters are always pressed for time. A variety of factors have made individual stories less valuable – so reporters must work on multiple pieces at once, and no matter what they do, it's always surpassed by the next big story. The best thing you can do is deliver the information they need as quickly as possible with the least amount of hassle.

One final thought: When a reporter asks a question, they want a direct answer. Never encourage anyone in your agency to "message" outside the question. If a hostile question comes your way, simply say: "Your underlying premise seems to be X. Let me explain why it's Y."

In more than a decade of federal service, I have found that most negative coverage has to do with the perception that

the agency is not forthcoming with the truth. Simply give
them the information they need – good, bad or indifferent –
respect their deadlines, and explain your limitations.

XVII

Self-Management

79

Stop Complaining About Your Indecisive Boss

It is one of the biggest frustrations people have with the government, with the workplace, with their loved ones, significant others and even with themselves—the inability to simply make a decision:

- "I do not understand how they can sit and sit and sit on that legislation."
- "I wrote that article months ago, and it's still sitting in her office."
- "We've been dating for four years now. He still won't make a commitment!"
- "I don't know what I should major in. There's just so much pressure!"

Of course, the more invested you are in the person or situation affected by indecisiveness, the worse the emotions surrounding it.

But the truth is, as bad as all of this is, that real pain doesn't come from other people's indecisiveness. You know very well that you can never control what others feel, think or do; that looking outside yourself for inner meaning, joy and purpose is worse than irrational. It's actually self-destructive.

If we've learned nothing else from pop psychology over the past 50 years, we have absorbed this: The only person you can control is you.

So complaining about other people's behavior, including their indecisiveness, is worse than a waste of time.

It masks the real problem, which is that *you* are the indecisive one.

You are delegating to another your inherent responsibility to make tough choices. It's easier to blame someone else for failing to do things right. But life is pretty harsh that way. It's set up to make us all walk the path at some point.

We won't get away without confronting them—the choices we never wanted to make. The ones we find most confusing, most complex, most heart-wrenching.

It's appropriate to think about this election year, how we get so caught up in blaming other people. If only they'd done this, if only they'd say that, if only they knew what they were doing. But these mind games don't fool anyone and they don't help any cause that I'm aware of, either.

Instead of waiting forever for indecisive others, you can make a decision, right now, today. If your life isn't working, change it. Let everybody else worry about themselves.

When you take your power back and make a decision, you have peace of mind. Even if you fail.

For "they" proceed as they will anyway, for a million reasons that have nothing to do with you.

The truth is, you do not have to think about, worry about,

or focus on the rest of the world. Not anymore. The only person you need to manage is you.

80

How to Call Out a Jerk at Work

I once asked my boss how he dealt so well with difficult people.

"I just think to myself, no matter how they scowl at me, I should not take it personally. Most likely they are having a very bad day." To which I responded, "But when is it enough?"

"What do you mean?" he responded. "When is it appropriate to call out an a-hole?"

"Oh boy," said my boss. "Gee whiz." He closed the door. Then he started to laugh, and tried to suppress it. "Please, please, please do not ever call out someone you think is an a-hole."

He looked at me intently. "In fact, you shouldn't even say the word."

"Why not?"

"Because if you call someone that name, they will surely find out that you said it."

"Oh."

Is that how we make decisions about things? Based on who might know that I think their behavior is unacceptable? Based on saving my own skin?

"Like I told you, just say to yourself, 'that person is surely having a very bad day, and their attitude has nothing to do with me.'"

I understood what my boss was saying. I did and I do—you don't want to alienate anybody at work. Anybody. What my boss was saying was that relationships at work are primary. If there is friction between you and another person, the work itself won't get done at all.

I appreciate that. But at the same time, when you smooth over unacceptable behavior, you are facilitating emotional harm to yourself and others. Even if this doesn't bother you morally, the result is guaranteed to be a loss of money—through conflict, disengagement and turnover. Not to mention the poor decisions that the hostile person forces onto others through irrational work processes, ill-thought out decisions, misdirected and incorrect communication. Then there's the hostility, vented like a broken steam-pipe wherever they go.

Who is responsible for stopping a jerk at work? The correct answer is: Everybody.

The job of a leader, and his or her executive team, is to model the appropriate tone—we respect other people around here. Management, in turn, implements the principles of leadership: Because we don't tolerate abusive people, we're going to establish processes that minimize or eliminate their impact on the workplace. The employee, it follows, is fully empowered to articulate appropriate boundaries: Yes, I will be diplomatic and supportive to my colleagues, but no I am not paid to serve as a punching bag.

Unfortunately, the world is sorely lacking in the great

leaders of yesteryear. It's become politically incorrect to simply put your foot down, and hold yourself and other people accountable.

But still, we can control ourselves. And that begins with a personal moral compass. When dealing with a jerk at work, it really doesn't matter if they've had a bad day. You say:

- "No I can't do that for you, sorry."
- "You just yelled. That is not appropriate when you're talking to me."
- "No, I don't agree to this proposed course of action, because it is inefficient. Even though you are insisting we follow it."

Of course, you never, ever descend to the level of becoming a jerk yourself. For example, it's not okay to call somebody names. But it is entirely appropriate to stand between their venom and your own self, and if you can, everybody else. It's the right thing to do, and the healthy thing to do.

Plus, when you look at the costs of mopping up the damage, forestalling jerky behavior saves the organization a ton of money.

XVIII

Social Media

81

The Real Problem For Bureaucracies On Social Media

It's a question that comes up a lot when organizations consider how to use social media most effectively: "How should we present our identity to the public?"

Here are the typical options, along with the pros and cons:

A single account where nobody knows who is talking (a.k.a. The Wizard of Oz): The benefit of this approach is that the organization does not risk its brand on the reputation of any one individual. On the other hand, social media is all about individuality and authenticity, so having an unnamed entity issuing messages is incongruous, to say the least.

A single organizational account explicitly populated by a staff, with messages identified by name: This approach humanizes the brand, but there is a lack of consistency in terms of "voice."

An individual account in the corporate name where the person is identified as a brand representative: This approach can be extremely successful, but if a popular social media representative leaves the team, that unique individuality is

313

suddenly absent, creating an identity problem for the brand.

An individual communicating as themselves, who is understood to be synonymous with the organization: This is typically the scenario when a senior executive communicates, and that person is so identified with their organization that the public understands they are "on duty" at all times. The problem of course is that we are all human, we all have private and public selves and it is unworkable in the long-term to expect any person to suppress their real selves for the sake of the organization.

An alternative approach is for the organization to create and re-create the brand in dialogue with its audience 24/7.

This means that there is no official social media presence for the brand. Rather, the organization allows the public to have its own authentic conversation about the brand without attempting to interfere.

In this scenario, the company or organization assumes that its own employees will participate in the conversation, but they will do so of their own volition, in their own voices, expressing themselves naturally and authentically without having to get approval for their messages first.

I realize that this is an unusual way for most organizations to think about social media but I think that it would address one of the most significant reasons that the public distrusts institutions, which is that they attempt to participate in communication in a manner that is forced and artificial.

By putting employees and other stakeholders on a level playing field, and essentially vacating any official stance on what should be a fully individualized set of platforms, the organization shows that it understands the inherent nature of this type of communication channel.

An organization's website is the only place it should anonymously provide official data and statements of position. These items belong to the corporate body, and no name need be attached to them. The focus should be on providing comprehensive information that is accessible, rich, and easy to navigate.

As with everything in life, the most important thing is to think before you do. Just because "everybody" has a social media account does not mean your organization needs to copy them.

82

What The Public Wants From A Government Twitter Account

I'm going to go out on a limb here and say that the average citizen feels like they don't know what the hell is going on in Washington.

I feel fairly confident in drawing this conclusion because every time, or nearly every time I talk to someone outside the Beltway they say something like this to me:

"Well I don't know what the hell is going on over there in Washington, maybe you can explain it to me."

And most of the time when I talk to people inside the Beltway, who don't work in my agency, my office, or my division I hear the same thing, well sorta:

"What exactly do you guys do over there?"

And then we start talking and...MEGO (my eyes glazeth over).

It's not like we government people don't try to explain. We do. But it's hard to do, and when we try to say it simply while also balancing the things we can and can't say, the result is usually less than compelling.

But the truth is that government work is fascinating, as we employees find ourselves:

- Navigating myriad layers of oversight – laws, regulations, guidelines, policies and rules to follow, plus organizational politics and culture.
- Struggling to simplify and clarify one's purpose – while answering to multiple audiences with varying kinds of interest in the mission and different levels of sophistication.
- Retaining stability in a chaotic environment – what was high-priority one day may disappear off the radar the next.

So why can't we tell that story? Why can't the public simply ask their questions and get the information they want?

Here's a "top 10" list of reasons that come to mind.

1. We can't tell them, and we don't explain why.
2. We can tell them, but we think we can't, because we're ignorant.
3. We promote "chain of command" thinking, in which mindset the customer has no choice but to take what we give them.
4. We prioritize operations over customer service.
5. We feel queasy about the kind of free social media tools that can help, because they raise uncomfortable questions.
6. We lack an accurate radar for the kinds of communication that are more versus less important.
7. We underfund the communication function.

8. We don't sufficiently empower and encourage subject matter experts to speak directly.
9. We are fearful of making an error in judgment or issuing inaccurate data.
10. We take so long to decide what to say, or how to say it, that people stop caring. (There is inevitably a vast gap between "*what we meant to say*" and "*what actually gets said*" –> once the Committee of All Relevant Parties is done with it.)

It is in this context that a government Twitter account becomes a valuable source of timely, relevant, understandable and accessible information for the public.

There are five kinds of Tweets that seem to generate the most impact:

1. Genuinely meaningful real-time status update
2. Direct quote that sheds light on what an influencer is thinking or planning.
3. Inspiring quote that sheds light on an influencer's vision
4. Statistic relevant to public policy
5. A visual that makes plain why an effort, initiative, or idea is important

A Twitter account can and should be used to tell the public what's going on, in real time. We have found that when we post cute pictures we get some retweets, but the number of follows and retweets explodes when we satisfy the public's true thirst.

The people want information that helps them to be informed citizens.

It is true that people get angry at government even in the best of scenarios. They're angry at corruption, they're angry at lack of accountability, they're angry at fraud, waste and abuse.

They are angry at lying.

But there is so much information that the public has a right to know, that can be shared, that would convey the sensitivity and the complexity of government work and actually promote engagement with government.

When we don't even bother to tell *that* story, in a way that people want to hear it, we are virtually guaranteed that citizens will, in thinking of the government, favor their worst fears.

Twitter is a revolutionary tool. We ought to take advantage of it, and of other free and low-cost technology platforms.

We should share as much information as we can.

Make sure it's marked clearly as originating from the government.

Invite others to share on our platforms.

Make clear the limits of our communication.

We should overall prioritize transparency and accountability to the fullest. Even when it makes us look bad.

The public may never love the government. But at the very least they should trust that government is working on its behalf.

Social media can help.

XIX

Training

83

Why Most Training Doesn't Work

We spend a lot of money on training. Most of the time, that money is wasted.

Let's start with the conferences, retreats, and weekends out of town. This includes Ted Talks, SXSW and all that other good stuff. Mostly it's a lot of crap from an actual learning perspective. Because officially approved case studies, no matter how compelling the subject matter, are normally sanitized to death. Because, of course, we don't embarrass ourselves; we're here to tell a positive story; we don't want to burn our bridges; the organization would have a massive fit if they found out you were telling us about that disaster; and so on.

Mostly these things are about big companies selling stuff, by getting smart and moneyed and influential people together. It's about saying, "I was there and I met XYZ and heard that." Of course it's about trying to network as well, and get a better job.

I remember one training conference in particular, one session in particular, where the speaker had so much to say, clearly. But it was equally clear that we would never get anything substantial out of him, because of confidentiality issues. Frustrated, I listened to the other audience members ask difficult questions, only to see the speaker do a kind of thrust-and-parry.

After the session I sat outside in the luxuriously decorated convention area and watched people form a line for little pastries, ask where the restroom was, flip up their laptops and mill about the vendor tables looking for free trinkets to take home.

Life-Changing Exceptions

Of course, some speakers will turn your entire career around. They are so dynamic, and they don't give a damn about sanitizing the story. They have the wonderful ability to actually tell you the truth. When you get to witness a talk like that, your life will never be the same.

For me one such experience was a 2003 "boot camp" sponsored by Ragan Communications. I had just started working for the government as an internal communicator, and my main job was to help write the monthly newsletter.

The main speaker at that event was employee communications expert Steve Crescenzo. Like many brilliant people he came off as absolutely crazy, this bald guy waving around really bad newsletters from various Fortune 500 companies and saying they were winning his "C.R.A.P. Awards."

The one thing that stuck with me from that training event was Crescenzo's passion for the subject matter. I think it is fair to say he was on a kind of moral crusade against bad writing and fluff writing—writing that wastes people's time.

A dozen years later, it is Crescenzo's ethic that informs my work as I write for the U.S. government. The writing here has gotten better, but the tendency toward C.R.A.P. remains. What Crescenzo helped me see is that fighting useless garbage words is a kind of war, and that even a single compromise of the keyboard has a domino effect.

We can't afford to let up, not even for a minute. Because then we've drunk the Kool-Aid, and even a little bit spreads through your body and to others, poisoning everyone in the system.

I also had the good fortune to attend a solo seminar by Shel Holtz, Crescenzo's one-time training partner at Ragan, on social media communication. When they use the word "guru" they are talking about him: He told us what mattered and why we should care about it, and then he told us what to do based on time-tested best practice. Many years later, his words are as accurate as they were when he uttered them.

The most important lesson I learned from Holtz was that in social media, you do not control the conversation but can only hope to be a valued part of it. The second most important thing is that you aren't required to tell everything, but you must say as much as you can. And then tell your audience explicitly, "we simply cannot share any further information at this time."

Every single minute of that seminar was vital to my professional life, and I burned those words into my brain like they had been applied by a branding iron.

The Limits of Online Training

But life-changing teachers are few and far between. And the training business—like the higher education business—is potentially very lucrative. So just as in higher education, online training has become a popular alternative to in-person events.

Theoretically, you can see where this makes economic sense. The problem however is that few people are actually going to learn anything by listening to the equivalent of Siri for an hour. So you've taken work time and exposed people to words uttered by a computer screen. It feels like progress, but is it?

Most of the time, I don't think so. That is, unless:

- You genuinely want to learn the subject matter and can't get to a live training class.
- Your job requires you to learn the information or get penalized in some way.
- Your professional advancement requires that you master new and unfamiliar subject matter, and you need to use online resources to teach yourself.

Take Six Sigma, for example. In my environment they use Six Sigma terms a lot, and so I found a free training class online that offered an introductory "white belt" in exchange for viewing the modules for a few minutes. I was motivated.

Unfortunately however, I did not have any specific tasks at work that I could tie the unusual jargon to. And the history of the discipline had no meaning to me. But I was invested intellectually in this journey, and so I read the information—again and again.

Will I get an advanced degree as a result of taking that class? No way. But do I have a somewhat better understanding of the subject, why it matters and how to apply it? Absolutely.

And when it comes to technical subjects like computer programming, online training is in my view an absolute must. I can't begin to count the number of people I know who are self-taught on coding, Web development, and graphic design, generally through a combination of work assignments and supplemental self-guided courses.

Disaster: Where Real Learning Happens

Even with all of this said, we haven't touched upon the most important way people learn stuff applicable to jobs, to relationships, to anything important in life. Most of us learn as a result of crisis: Failure, screwups, just plain getting it wrong and embarrassing ourselves in the process.

I'll never forget my first fashion faux pas in summer camp, when I approached the rich girls from Long Island and complimented their designer clothing. *"You can't even pronounce Benetton," said one of them. "Ewwww you."*

There was the pain of transitioning from a private-sector, self-promotional environment to the low-key, conservative world that is a government agency. *"Where did you come from? Are you aware that this is the government?"*

The realization that my assumptions about being a parent have very little to do with what is actually necessary for parenting, and everything to do with making up for the mistakes I perceived my parents to have made. *"Mom, do me a favor, would you let me cross the street by myself just once in a while?"*

Learning Techniques of the Resilient

Each of us, of course, has a large collection of failures and it's up to us to decide what we do with the impact they have on our lives.

Here are the tactics that don't work:

Some people put their heads down. They get depressed. They hate themselves. They remind themselves what losers they are, how they never have been any better and how they probably never will be better.

Others just don't really think about it. They continue in their routines, trying to avoid making another similar mistake in the future—effectively crossing the street because they tripped in a particular spot.

Still others assign blame to the people around them, to their bosses, to their parents, to their significant others, to their life situations, to the placement of the moon, or to the weather—anything as long as they don't have to be responsible, figure it out or fix it.

But the people who survive and move on do something else.

They are the ones who fail but have the capacity to stop and break the problem down. Because it is through crisis that they come to understand the problem. It is through a rupture in the system that they can retrace their steps, and ultimately find remedies.

What were the steps that got me into this mess? They ask. Never mind who's at fault, how can I fix it?

They make a list—Step 1, Step 2, Step 3 and this is how I got here. And then they take a look at all the resources available to help them fix it.

They read. They talk to friends. They make a game plan for change. They establish small milestones for progress as part of the game plan. And they ask other people for support.

Every single day, every person faces crises big and small. Every single day we fail and fall and are embarrassed at the smallness of our minds, at our limited capacity. And every single day we have the choice. We can learn our way through the problem. We can get up.

84

Why Plain Language Training Lacks Teeth

My daughter taught me a Taoist saying:

"Beautiful words are not true, and the truth is not beautiful."

There are many reasons why government writing is not plain. Only one of them has to do with skill:

1. Confused thinking
2. Lack of critical thinking
3. Lazy thinking – you pass the buck to the reader to figure it out
4. Jargon has replaced standard style guide – e.g. "writing for ourselves then pretending everyone else should understand"
5. Legalistic approach – "give them all the raw data and that way we're not interpreting it for them" – and can't get in trouble
6. Executive preference
7. Public Affairs type "messaging" replaces substantive

    information or Public Affairs can censor

8. Unrealistic deadline or insufficient staff
9. Lack of collaboration, stove piping – e.g. "Stay out of my business"
10. Communication is one person's job vs. everyone's
11. Writing not exposed to broad audience for critical review
12. Insulation from negative feedback
13. Worse consequences for providing bad news clearly than for muddling the information or making it less accessible
14. Clear communication seen as too simple – "Reads like USA Today"
15. Writing for professor of economics not 8th graders
16. Fear of misinterpretation, intentional or not; fear of negative press
17. Fear of getting in trouble or losing one's job for conveying bad news
18. Lack of ability to use visual aids when appropriate
19. Communication staff is operational rather than communication-focused
20. History or context of the information is omitted deliberately so as not to raise further questions

Plain language training is only partly useful to address the above. In fact one could argue it is a panacea used to divert attention from the real issues.

XX

Technology

85

How Over-Customization Kills Government Technology

Yesterday Scott Burns, the CEO and founder of GovDelivery (disclaimer: not an endorsement) published "The Elephant in the Room…Is Government the Worst Possible Customer?" on LinkedIn.

As someone who has worked for the government for more than a dozen years, and who frequently helps define requirements for government IT projects, I was interested to hear a vendor's idea of the things that are taboo to say.

His list of reasons why venture capitalists shy away from government as a customer include: 1) excessive customization requirements; 2) excessively cost-based decision-making; and 3) excessive paperwork.

Overall I agree with Burns' assessment, and hope that the next administration will take on the challenges he outlines. It will not be an easy undertaking, for the following reasons:

- Excessive customization requirements are a mask for self-interest. Frankly, many departments, functions, and jobs are outdated and even superfluous. Commitment to a true commercial-off-the-shelf IT solution, together with the adoption of private-sector best practices, makes that obvious.

- Excessive cost-based decision making is a mask for self-interest. The government has a notoriously high IT project failure rate for many reasons, chief among which is the ignorance and risk-aversion of those writing contract requirements. If you know your stuff, you aren't afraid to specify what a quality solution is. If you don't, you can always defend your decision by saying it was the cheapest. In the end, such thinking is always just the opposite—a costly mistake.
- Excessive paperwork is a mask for self-interest. Government contracting is currently a nightmarish field of endeavor. I have known some outstanding professionals who work in this area and all of them were unusually well-schooled in the law and also unusually thick-skinned when it came to dealing with the sharks inside and outside the agency who relentlessly pursued their own agenda and financial self-interest regardless of whether it benefited the agency's mission.

In my view, it is unnecessary to implore individual government professionals to solve these problems. Rather, we have to take a sledgehammer to the structural incentives that enable them to persist.

Regardless of who we work for, I think most people can agree on the very basic idea that government exists to serve the taxpayer. The taxpayers do not exist to prop up a bloated, inefficient and self-serving bureaucracy.

86

When a Shortcut Means Shortchanging Yourself

There in the corner of my childhood kitchen in New Jersey sat a small, nondescript plywood shelf virtually stuffed with oddly shaped purple boxes. The boxes contained a magical potion called the Cookie Diet, and when I was growing up in New Jersey we sold a ton of them.

Do you remember this? A "delicious chocolate-chip cookie for breakfast, one for lunch and a healthy dinner," or something like that. People went insane. I can have my cookies and lose weight too? Unbelievable!

But we always struggled with our weight in the family, because food = love. Nevertheless we tried.

In its purest form ("induction") the Atkins plan will also make you lose weight. But it is absolutely disgusting. You're supposed to be able to eat "whatever you want" from a menu of delicious food. The problem is, your body wasn't made to live on a dozen eggs a day plus oil, cheese and cream, platefuls of steak and chicken and liver spread. Sure, you lose weight. But the last time I tried it, my cholesterol shot up to 450, because all I wanted to eat was hard salami.

If there is a shortcut to be found, be sure that my family has tried it.

We were big fans of all the gadgets they sold on TV, to make every aspect of life easier. You know which ones I mean—"As Seen On TV" in the mall:

- Flat blue plastic things with long extensions, for folding laundry quickly.
- The oven that makes an entire chicken on the stovetop, no mess, no fuss.
- Wallets that hold all thirty of your credit cards, ID cards, loyalty cards, and folded-up slips of paper with your reminders in them.
- The chemical that makes any fabric super clean.
- A wipey that gets your car as shiny as it was the day you bought it.

Goodness gracious, shortcuts.

My Zayde, may he rest in peace, was famous for two things: kosher liver knishes (you had to taste them to believe) and the first kosher TV dinners in Toronto, so that the women could go to work and—you guessed it—serve a shortcut to a "real, homemade" dinner.

As a child, my IQ tested high and so I skipped a grade. Nice shortcut.

One time I had a teacher whose borderline creepy behavior was enough to send my mother into the principal's office and my father to the school board. They moved me up a grade rather than deal with him. That is called a "workaround."

I went to a college that accepted transfer credit based on

life experience, got some of my master's credits online, and did my dissertation on soap operas because that was the only primary material I could get my hands on while raising two kids.

Shortcuts, shortcuts, shortcuts.

I remember shopping for designer clothes on the clearance rack, every Sunday with my mom. You can have designer clothes but not pay designer prices. How smart!

Shortcuts are essentially "life hacks." They are so popular nowadays it seems almost a cardinal sin to question them. But we shortchange ourselves when we jump from rung to rung like animals.

There was a book I had as a child. I can't remember the name of it now. The main characters were a little girl and a little boy who lived in a forest. They get their hands on a ball of string with magical properties—the more you pull it the older you get.

Of course the children were curious. They tugged at it a little and then couldn't stop themselves, wanting to know what would come next in life. So impatient. Why wait?

Suddenly they are old people.

Somehow they wish they'd never found the magic.

We live in the Age of Technology now (or is it the Age of Anxiety?) and perhaps a desire to slow down and think things through is mostly impossible.

But I wonder if we would be happier.

What if we really read a book and just enjoyed it? Really took it in, instead of scanning dozens of feeds a day for more, more, more information? What if we made our own food, as in cooking? What if we actually sewed? What if we just stopped trying to be so "smart?"

I saw a dad with his son the other day, just kicking a soccer ball back and forth. The father was really interacting with the kid. He was talking to him, happily and seemingly in no rush. No cellphone anywhere.

My mind flew back to all the piano lessons, dance recitals, theater rehearsals, gym beam practices and other activities of my childhood. In their zeal to cram every possible developmental activity into my life, in the shortest possible time, my parents deprived me of the only thing I ever really wanted: Time with them. Attention.

What I saw on that soccer field was that thing. I cried a lot that day, the kind of tears that other people will never understand. Not everything in life can be bought, sold, condensed, hacked, traded, automated, and served up like a McDonald's Happy Meal.

Some things have to be slow in order to be real. In order to be lived.

Life is so very precious, and short.

Living it is better than a bad shortcut.

87

10 Typical Concerns About Social Intranets

I am not suggesting that these are right or wrong, only that they represent the kinds of things people say. I am also not suggesting that having concerns is inherently a bad thing. In every single organization I have worked for, some variation on these themes has come up.

1. "If they (employees) have an open forum and complain about something, we will be liable if we don't fix it."
2. "They will complain nonstop. Especially the troublemakers."
3. "They will spend all day talking about nothing, instead of doing their work."
4. "The union will be all over us."
5. "Do you know how many (legal, IT security, HR…) issues this brings up?"
6. "And who is going to staff this thing?"
7. "What is the authoritative version? What if someone puts out misinformation?"

8. "If the employees can just communicate with one another, what do they need communicators for?"
9. "Work is not social. Work is work."
10. "I don't understand why they can't just use email."

My own personal view is that the more evolved your leadership and management culture is, the less likely you are to hear these kinds of things. Because the workplace of the future is essentially about a geographically distributed small team, collaborating within a larger network, to get things done. Open communication promotes trust, and trust promotes collaboration.

Of course the elephant in the room is = what happens when we are so productive with so few resources and such high technology that we simply don't need as many staff? And don't need the traditional hierarchical management style (read: SES jobs and excessive layers of middle management). What happens when people simply join the civil service, self-organize, pick a project, and check in with compliance experts to make sure they are following the law?

I can't answer that, but economic realities will force us to ask the question

88

The 10 Essential Tasks Of A Knowledge Manager

Nobody wants to think about knowledge management, but everybody needs it. Here are the basic things an organization should have covered as part of its KM system.

1. Establishing an information architecture for multiple user groups, permission levels, and knowledge sharing environments
2. Maintaining the architecture, adding and removing people from user groups
3. Locating and archiving institutional knowledge
4. Establishing taxonomies, workflow systems, approval systems so that we know which documents are approved for release and who the audiences are for that release
5. Ensuring compliance with reporting requirements
6. Ensuring everyone can find the information they need quickly and that the most recent version is online.
7. Version control.
8. Upgrading the collaboration environment as new tech-

nologies come online

9. Exploring efficient new technologies and incorporating them where practical
10. Teaching users to use more advanced features associated with collaboration platforms, like mapping a drive, establishing a workflow, etc.

89

The Solution Is Big Data

"Spin" means intentionally misleading the audience so as to persuade them (propaganda). This is NOT OK for government to do – unless you're in the military doing psychological operations overseas as part of war.

In all my years in the federal government, I have never – not once – had someone tell me to lie or mislead. EVER. If that were to happen I would report it and you should too. I have read about such occurrences though. Normally they leak into social media, and then into regular media if there's overwhelming credibility to the story. That said:

–My experiences is that agencies are responsive rather than proactive. They wait for the question. They are not hanging around waiting to air what they perceive as dirty laundry. It is often frustrating to me personally as a communicator that we don't get more in line with the private sector, where there is a pretty good understanding that when you share bad news very early on, it loses impact. (Best example is David Letterman who rebounded right away from his PR crisis by simply acknowledging his personal mistakes.)

–It is standard practice to answer the question you were asked. Not more, not less. We are working in a legal environment where words have tremendous impact. Washington is not a TV talk show. Words are chosen carefully not spontaneously and they are done in conformity with numerous legal requirements – including Plain Language.

–I have heard SMEs (subject matter experts) say to writers, "Put your spin on this." However, what they usually mean is – "Here are the facts. I know I can't write. Make them sound better." It is a way of acknowledging their limitations. Sometimes it's a way of acknowledging that the data sounds bad. But keep in mind that government words are cleared through various officials so it would be very hard to simply "spin something" without a huge team of people on board. Normally those people are pointing out how the content could be more accurate, more clear.

All of that said–

The problem with narrative is narrative itself. Every agency and every company has to describe in a narrative fashion what they are doing. And as nobody and no organization is perfect there will always be delicate subjects. Nobody is going to run around saying, "Look how we screwed up today! Woo-hoo!" That would be ridiculous and a waste of time – just as phony feelgood stories are. Not all of it is high value.

This is why the emphasis on narrative is misplaced.

The best way out of the "messaging" trap is BIG DATA.

Simply make high-value data sets available in an accessible manner. Let the relevant facts speak for themselves. Officials can offer their comments, but the data is the most important thing.

90

50% Of Your Salary To Write Emails: Are You Worth It?

Private-sector survey research published in 2011 by Inc. Magazine found that employees of small to medium-size businesses spend about 50% of their time on email. (Here's the press release.)

(It's not actually fully 50% if you read the survey results carefully – because there is an element of phone messaging involved – but let's just take that as a ballpark figure for discussion.)

I would also take as a ballpark figure the findings of the research sponsor, which (unsurprisingly) has a "unified communications" product to sell that supposedly eliminates the inefficiency caused by relying so much on email. So they make big claims like:

"Efficiencies created by Unified Communications on a typical firm with 50 Knowledge Workers (sic) with salaries ranging from $40,000 to $110,000....(are) valued at approximately $950,000 annually."

Yet despite the inevitable bias and hype, their findings resonate with my own experience. Email is a costly waste of time when you have the option of working in a collaboration environment.

In particular I find this to be true of Google's collaboration tools – Docs and Sites. It takes a little bit of getting used to, but compared with the frustration of trying to do things in an Outlook environment the learning curve is well worth it.

(As always, this is personal opinion – not endorsed or sponsored.)

What the heck are people doing on email (and phone) all day? According to Fonality's survey:

- 36% – trying to contact people, find information, or schedule a meeting.
- 14% – "duplicating information" – forwarding emails, etc. – or managing unwanted communication (spam emails and phone calls)

Think about it:

- The median salary of a CEO in the United States is about $725K.
- The average lawyer's salary spans between $44-$171K.
- The average salary of a federal employee is $75K.

Are you worth half your salary in email?

What will you do when your boss catches on that all the email is largely a waste of time?

Although it is a difficult thing to do when seemingly "everybody" uses email, my suggestion would be to get ahead of the curve and transition to collaboration-based work now. The result:

- In the short-term, you will hate it because you have to evangelize a lot.
- In the medium-term you will find yourself happier because you save yourself time and aggravation associated with mindlessly forwarding, detaching, and reattaching email – not to mention the inaccuracies associated with "who had the latest version of that?"
- In the longer-term, spending a larger proportion of your time on actual knowledge work is a much better way to demonstrate value to your organization than email-pushing.

XXI

Trust

91

How Poor Government Communication Strategy Fuels Paranoia

By and large, Americans in 2017 have a fairly negative perception of government. And it's far worse than it was 20 years ago. The government's failure to adapt its communication approach to reality is only making things worse.

Let's take a look at some data.

A Pew Research Center survey of 1,501 adults age 18 and older nationwide, conducted April 5–11, 2017, asked people to pick the phrase that best describes their feelings about the government: "basically content," "frustrated," or "angry." To enable a comparison of data over time, Pew has repeated this survey annually.

Since 1997, the likelihood of describing oneself as "frustrated" has remained pretty much static, at slightly more than half (55 percent now, 56 percent then). But the likelihood of calling oneself "basically content" with the government is statistically much lower, with 29 percent choosing this word in 1997 versus only 19 percent in 2017. Meanwhile, the level of anger has nearly doubled in 20 years, from 12 percent to 22 percent.

Survey respondents don't trust "the government in Washington to do what is right," and their fondness for "the swamp" is diminishing speedily. In 1997, fully 39 percent said they trusted government integrity "always/most of the time." But 20 years later, that credibility, which could be viewed as brand equity, has diminished to just 20 percent.

Mistrust of the government, of course, is part and parcel of American culture. The classic essay collection "Why People Don't Trust Government" points out three obvious reasons for the declining trust: "Age-old suspicion of authority"; the "sense that politicians have lost their dignity"; and a "deeper set of accumulated grievances with political authority, institutions and processes in general."

The book was published in 1997, before the drop in citizen trust and contentment documented by Pew's annual survey. It was around this time that social media began to take off. And there can be little doubt that this technology, by enabling citizens to engage with one another and respond to authority, has compounded the problem of mistrust in government.

It's hard to say for sure when exactly social media went mainstream. But the first bulletin board systems were online by the 1970s, and forums, newsgroups, instant messaging, and other forms of peer-to-peer communication continued to proliferate. By 1999, the Cluetrain Manifesto captured the spirit of the day:

> *"Whether explaining or complaining, joking or serious,*
> *the human voice is unmistakably genuine . . . Most*

> *corporations, on the other hand, only know how to talk in the soothing, humorless monotone of the mission statement, marketing brochure, and your-call-is-important-to-us busy signal. Same old tone, same old lies.*"

As social media picked up steam, corporate, not-for-profit, academic and government leaders alike were confronted with a growing demand for immediate and thorough answers to their questions. As organizational consultant Gavin Rouble has pointed out, their tendency has been to do one of two ineffective things in response. One tactic is to "interpret being questioned as an attack on them," and instead of answering the question, "attacking the person who raised the question." Another is to "answer the question without actually answering."

Regardless of the reason for ineffective government communications, the result is the same: a not-very-tasty (to the citizen) layer cake, where feelgood efforts are the most prominent, and the unpalatable, difficult to handle, social-media-driven conversations are not only de-prioritized, they're left out of the cake altogether.

In the middle of the cake, there is visible compliance-driven reporting, but it's hard to get people excited about complicated data that doesn't always result in a good news story.

There is also a layer dedicated to customer service: In 2011, then-President Obama issued an Executive Order mandating improvements in this area, noting that "the public deserves competent, efficient, and responsive service from the Federal Government. Executive departments and agencies must continuously evaluate their performance in meeting this standard and work to improve it."

Yet in 2017, the energy around customer service, from my experience and observation, remains at the individual level. Though there appears to be forward movement on a number of fronts (for example through the use of artificial intelligence-driven avatars), there remains a systemic problem with handling complex inquiries in multiple languages with personalized and satisfactory resolution in a timely manner—the sort of thing citizens have come to expect from successful mass retailers, such as Amazon.

Open data was the subject of another Executive Order, issued in 2013, and the Office of Management and Budget issued a Memorandum outlining the expectation that government data would be issued in open, machine-readable format. In a relatively short time (meaning the past several years) the General Services Administration's Technology Transformation Service has made a number of strides toward improving citizen's experience with government by leveraging open data. See, for example, the work of its 18F unit with the Federal Election Commission.

However, open data is still, for the most part, not a concept that most government communication shops see as integral to their missions. The graphic below, which I produced, shows the result of ineffective government communication strategy, using the layer cake analogy.

The U.S. government should have a clear and well thought out communication strategy, based on communication standards that stand regardless of which political party is in power. (Full disclosure: I co-authored a research paper on this issue for the Federal Communicators Network, for which

I volunteer.)

The strategy should be updated annually, and success should be measured according to a clear set of goals and objectives. The U.K. has done this for several years.

Until the U.S. formally develops a strategy, we can establish a general, citizen-centered framework that takes into account the realities of today's social attitudes toward government.

The graphic below shows what this might look like: Responses to social media grace the top of the cake, followed by customer service, then open data, then compliance reporting, and finally outreach efforts based primarily on making citizens aware of the products and services they are entitled to.

The bottom line is this: Citizens are more educated and empowered than ever.

At the same time, their perceptions of government are deeply negative, and the situation is not getting better.

As such, if the government does not adapt effectively, citizen-to-citizen communication will ultimately eclipse what federal officials have to say.

Moreover, mistrustful, angry and frustrated citizens are likely to misinterpret legitimate government communications as nefarious. The consequences of this misinterpretation include compounded hostility toward government, with myriad potential negative consequences. One of the most prominent among these is the tendency to favor unsourced "fake news" over accurate data.

The government can respond effectively to this situation by reversing its traditional approach to communication. In this framework, responding to social media is of critical and primary importance.

To make this shift effectively, the default attitude must be to communicate, even if it's to say that "we're not at liberty to say."

It goes without saying that corruption must be rooted out and eliminated regularly in order for any communication strategy to work.

92

When The Public Wants Information, Resistance Is Futile

In my nuclear family we never talked about controversial stuff. Basically, we handled conflict either by my mother saying "shhh" or my grandmother saying "shhh."

If a fight broke out, we simply didn't talk to one another. Three days was the minimum, a few months was the max. It was never clear how we would start talking again, because nobody believed in apologizing. But just as it began, it would be over and talking about whatever the fight was about was simply not allowed.

Joining the government more than a decade ago, I rapidly felt right at home.

"There is a problem with this program that the public should know about."

"Shhh."

"Someone is selling a service we provide for free, and charging $250."

"Shhh."

"Our technology is on eBay."

"Shhh."

"I have a Tweet I would like you to consider for your approval."

"I don't know what that is. Let me see the briefing book."

Once, a boss once even warned me that "they might question your loyalty if you continue to push them to talk."

"Shhh."

I programmed the electronic newsletter so that readers could give articles 1-5 star ratings. They made me take it down.

Another time, I said to the boss: "I still have no idea how your business model works, and if you can't explain it to me how can I possibly explain it to the world?"

"Shhh."

Maybe it's me. Maybe Gen Xers make everything into too big of a deal. Millennials and Generation Z are totally online, all the time. In fact they don't seem to have any concept of personal privacy or taboo topics. For them, it's all part of the same newsfeed. So I have to believe that for those who seek information from the government going forward, there will be an attitude of expectation: "Of course you owe me all the information."

It won't be deferential as in the past. The public won't be saying, "Oh, it's okay, I heard you before when you said 'shhh.'"

Information is expected. The kids, and increasingly their parents, demand nothing less.

This is nothing short of a revolution.

We will see the public insist that government provide the highest levels of customer service, transparency, and yes, return on investment based on metrics.

It will be common for us to answer questions by Tweet, text, chat, email, telephone call, and even those little avatars that jump around the screen and anticipate what is wanted.

Times have changed. There is no such thing as avoiding the public because we don't like the questions or the expectations they are bringing us.

In a world where Google is a verb and not a noun, "shhh" just doesn't work anymore as a default answer from the government.

93

Law Enforcement and the Crisis of Public Confidence

"If You See Something, Say Something" is the most memorable public safety campaign I can think of. It began as a Homeland Security Department initiative but quickly branched out into a nationwide initiative at the federal, state and local levels and you can see the motto everywhere, particularly at public transportation hubs.

Here's a fun fact: the motto was originally rejected. As Mike Riggs reported several years ago in Reason.com (citing an Adweek article from 2002), Korey Kay & Partners tried to get the federal government to adopt it after the terrorist attacks of September 11, 2001. Nobody was interested — not DHS, not the Justice and State departments.

But eventually DHS did adopt it, and according to Riggs, in 2008 the line "went viral." (The article offers an excellent timeline showing key moments in its adoption.) The question for students of law enforcement communication, and social media marketing, is whether the campaign has actually worked. The consensus is that it hasn't:

- New York magazine writer Dwyer Gunn, citing the work of NYU sociologist Harvey Molotch, points to the detrimental effect of many "leads that are likely to amount to nothing." For one thing, they make each individual lead less likely to be taken seriously. Overall, he notes, the program "hasn't yielded any terrorists."
- The New York Times in 2008 noted that the New York Metropolitan Transit Authority (MTA) claimed it got 1,944 campaign-related tips in 2006. The result? "No terrorists were arrested, but a wide spectrum of other activity was reported."
- TechDirt.com called the campaign the creation of a "Massive Database Of Useless Info From Citizens Spying On Each Other."

These commentators may be right; perhaps encouraging people to report on suspicious activities mucks up the system, distracts the feds and the police, creates unnecessary delays, and encourages an atmosphere of suspicion.

But then again, perhaps the problem with the campaign was not the idea, but its execution. Terrorism is on the increase, not the decline, and we need all available information to fight it. In "Key Trends in the Uncertain Metrics of Terrorism," published in 2016 by the Center for Strategic & International Studies, Anthony H. Cordesman notes:

"Virtually all of the data available indicate that these threats to the United States and its allies remain critical and that the geographic scope and intensity of terrorism continues to increase. At the same time, there are critical problems and shortfalls in the data available, a

*near total lack of credible unclassified data on the cost
and effectiveness of various counterterrorism efforts,
and critical problems in the ways the United States
approaches terrorism."*

In short, what Cordesman is saying is that we don't know
enough, we don't measure well enough, and we don't think
smartly enough about how we fight the bad guys (and ladies).

The public can and should play a huge role in supporting
government efforts to fight terrorism. And despite the
widespread criticism it has received, a glitzy ad campaign like
"If You See Something, Say Something" can help. But — and
this is a big but — by failing to report studiously on results,
law enforcement leaves the public with the impression that
this is a superficial campaign.

It gets worse than that. While the public respects law enforcement, they have almost no trust in the institutions
and individuals associated with politics and public service.
So while Gallup found in 2016, for example, that 76% of
Americans have "a great deal of respect for the police." they
simultaneously learned that:

- Only 7% have "a great deal of trust and confidence" in
  those "who either hold or are running for public office."
- Only 22% had "a great deal of trust and confidence"
  in the Executive, Judicial and Legislative branches of
  government combined.
- And only 8% had "a great deal of trust and confidence" in
  the Federal government's handling of domestic problems;

11% said the same of international problems.

"If You See Something, Say Something" is a great idea. It's a great concept. It's a great ad and a great brand. But in order for a brand to work, its customers have to see a promise being kept.

Law enforcement should start to fulfill the promise of this campaign by focusing on its results. If they're getting too many useless leads, they should help the public deliver more fruitful ones. And they should provide regular progress reports, in a coordinated way, that show how these improvements are yielding a true return on investment for the public.

94

To Restore Trust In Government, Empower Federal Communicators

An October 2013 survey by the Pew Research Center for U.S. Politics & Policy found that most Americans (62 percent) had a positive view of federal workers, and a majority had a positive view of the federal agencies they were asked about. But few (19 percent) trusted the government itself "to do what is right just about always or most of the time."

Over the years I have received many email chains (Fwd: Fwd: Fwd:) portraying the government as corrupt or inefficient while hearing verbal anecdotes of federal employees who went the extra mile to help out.

Clearly, many federal employees are dedicated. The 2015 Federal Employee Viewpoint Survey, administered by the Office of Personnel Management, shows that more than 90 percent of respondents "view their work as important, are willing to commit extra effort when necessary to get their jobs done, [and] consistently seek out ways to do better."

Feds are also committed to integrity; they don't give you spin. Only 43 percent of respondents to the survey agreed that "senior leaders generate high levels of motivation and commitment in the workforce," and 55 percent agreed that "my organization's senior leaders maintain high standards of honesty and integrity."

The father of classical public relations, Edward Bernays—who propagandized for the U.S. government in favor of entering World War I—once famously wrote that "propaganda is the executive arm of the invisible government." But today, ambiguity around the nature and purpose of government messaging has in my view created the current environment of distrust.

A better course of action would be to charge Federal employees with disseminating government information in such a way that fact is clearly distinguished from message. This is the model followed by the UK, and we should adopt it here.

95

How Poor Communication Fosters Distrust in Government

People nowadays don't trust the government. Maybe you think they shouldn't trust the government. Frankly, sometimes I don't trust the government. And sometimes, unfortunately, that mistrust is well-placed. (Just pick up any newspaper.)

Most of the time, though, we government employees are a pretty decent bunch. Hardworking, honest, and we genuinely want to help. We want to make a difference, even if it's a small one. But something often gets in our way—we don't control the system.

To a much larger extent than people appreciate, the structure of society determines how the individuals within it behave. Imagine a country with ineffective, corrupt, or absent police. How would that affect your feelings and behaviors around self-defense? Or how about living under a religious dictatorship. Would religion be appealing?

Culture is a manifestation of structure. It is "the way we do things around here," and it reflects the values underpinning our system of law.

Back to government.

Often people lament the poor quality of government communication versus the private sector. In fact, the 2010 Plain Writing Act was passed as a way of addressing the problem, by "forcing" agencies to speak clearly.

Half a decade later, it remains routine for government-speak to be unintelligible to many. It is better, but we aren't close to there yet.

The reason government communication often leaves much to be desired? It has little to do with government writers and everything to do with structure—including the culture that stems from it.

The nature of government is to be relatively opaque about its activities. This is not a revolutionary statement but common sense. It's not just because of national security, it's a law of bureaucracy: All large, complex institutions easily become "too big to fail," motivated by a kind of self-sustaining survival instinct.

And thus the social function of Congress, the justice system, the media and various watchdog groups, whistleblowers and others is to force the government to be more transparent. As fraud, waste and abuse is "outed," bad practices have to stop because they simply cannot withstand public scrutiny.

This is the context in which the goal of government communication bears reconsidering.

The classical view is that the writers serve and reflect the agency in which they are situated. If the agency is turgid and obtuse, then guess what? So will the writing be.

But what if the job of a government writer were reconceived—as a tool to serve the public? It sounds almost insane to put it this way, right? Serving the taxpayer ought to be the first order of business. But let's be honest: It is difficult to extricate an agency's self-perpetuating tendencies from the mission it carries out. And employees will naturally reflect this inherent conflict, which makes it important for the agency itself to use communication as a corrective tool. Meaning, you don't operate in reactive mode, wasting resources fending off charges of poor stewardship after the fact.

Instead, you use the communication function as a diagnostic tool. You consider every single decision through the eyes of an impartial third party. Flowing from that approach, you design a comprehensive communication culture. People routinely think, talk and write from the perspective of "what would my mother think?" or "how would this look on the cover of the newspaper, above the fold?"

It sounds simple and obvious but in practice it is easy to make common sense complicated. You pack a lunch before you go to work with the idea that 10 minutes of preparation can save you $10 and a long line at the salad bar. In the same way, creating a culture of accountability, well in advance of any specific writing task, is the best way to invest in the communication function.

96

How To Restore Public Trust In Government – Without Paying A Single Cent

More than 3 out of 4 Americans don't trust the federal government.

- In 2014, only 24% of Americans said they trusted the government to do what's right "always or most of the time."
- Sixty years ago, in 1964, that figure was more than 50 percentage points higher – 77%. (Source: Pew Research Center, 2014)

Government leaders know that communication is a vital government function.

Recognizing this, nearly 20 years ago, in 1996, U.S. Vice President Al Gore formed the Federal Communicators Network.

> *"The Vice President's vision was to reach federal work-ers with important reinvention messages, promote a climate in which reinvention can flourish, and create a grass-roots demand to break down agency barriers to reinvention." (Source: National Partnership for Reinventing Government archive via University of North Texas Libraries and the Government Printing Office.)*

Unfortunately, however, the Vice President's vision was not realized.

In 2013, only 50.3% of the federal workforce was satisfied with the communication they receive from their leaders, per a Partnership for Public Service (PPS) analysis. They don't feel like they get enough information about:

- Goals and priorities
- News about the agency generally
- Information about what's happening outside their imme-diate sphere of work

For good employee communication to happen, says the PPS, it has to be a priority; it has to take place through a number of channels simultaneously; it has to be open and honest; and employee suggestions have to be taken into account.

The private sector is better than the government at this, says the PPS.

And not knowing what's going on obviously leaves people frustrated and unable to contribute fully to the mission.

It goes without saying, but is worth saying anyway, that:

- There is a statistically significant correlation between effective workplace communication and employee job satisfaction, but communicating effectively and motivating employees is a challenge for many leaders. (Deloitte Consulting LLP, "Silencing the static: Engaging employees in an unsettled environment," July 2014, via Partnership for Public Service)
- In an environment where internal transparency is scarce, effective external communication is more than challenging. It's impossible.

One might argue that we shouldn't rely on federal communicators: "Let the data speak for itself."

But that approach isn't working either. In 2015, 10 out of 12 (83.3%) federal agencies most frequently receiving FOIA requests failed to provide adequate access to government information. Again, it's not because federal employees are incompetent. Rather, according to the Center for Effective Government, the function is insufficiently funded, staffed, planned for and automated.

Poor communication and perceived corruption go hand-in-hand.

In 2014, the United States ranked #17 out of 100 on the perceived corruption index published by Transparency International. A score of 0 means "highly corrupt," vs. 100 means "very clean." According to TI, a poor score is likely a sign of widespread bribery, lack of punishment for corruption and public institutions that don't respond to citizens' needs.

There is hope in the form of improved compliance with the Plain Language Act of 2010. Earlier this year, the Center for Plain Language released its report card of federal agencies' compliance with the law requiring them to speak in language that most people can understand. On the whole, agencies have gotten better: 86% are in compliance with the law's requirements – up from only 54% just one year ago.

Improved readability not a small feat for agencies to have achieved. In an interview with Federal News Radio, government communications veteran and plain language volunteer Annetta Cheek said:

> *"The result looks easy, but getting there is not so easy. Writing bureaucratically is much easier."*

As someone who has worked in the federal government for more than a decade, I have observed firsthand the tendency to lean on bureaucratic writing as way out of dealing with un-comfortable, confusing, complex, and sensitive topic matter.

And have seen how the resulting confusion on the part of the public leads to the automatic assumption that the government must be doing something wrong; must be hiding the truth, because "they can't just come out and say what's going on."

It's also obvious to anyone who reads social media that a lack of ready access to information creates fertile soil for conspiracy theorists.

We can fix this problem by giving federal employees – not just communicators but all employees – significantly more information.

Federal employees are trustworthy, and they are trusted by the public.

According to The Pew Research Center, 62% of the public have a "favorable" view of federal employees, even as their trust in the government as a whole has plummeted.

I have also observed in my personal life that people frequently tell me positive stories about their one-on-one interactions with feds.

To improve trust in government, and to improve workplace productivity, agencies should arm employees with information and encourage them to communicate freely – anything that is not confidential.

Social media is effective as a communication tool precisely because of the power of uncensored word-of-mouth. Even when the news is bad, people trust the messenger who gives it to them straight.

Who better to share information through regular media and social media than the federal employee who is deeply familiar with their own workplace environment?

Fears that employees cannot be trusted with meaningful information are unfounded. Study after study shows that federal employees are extraordinarily dedicated, regardless of the trying circumstances.

As the Office of Personnel Management noted with regard to the 2014 Federal Employee Viewpoint Survey, which included 392,752 employees from 82 agencies, the vast majority of Federal employees believe their work is important, put in extra effort to get their jobs done and actively look for ways to do their jobs better. Seventy percent of respondents said that their work gives them a feeling of personal accomplishment.

Indeed, The Washington Post ran a story last December about Department of Homeland Security employees who said they'd stay on the job even if they had to work without a paycheck.

The path to increased return on investment for civil service salaries is clear and straightforward:

1. Boost communication with individual federal employ-
    ees.
2. Encourage individual federal employees to communicate
    with the public about what they know, as long as it's not
    confidential.
3. Watch the workplace satisfaction of feds increase.
4. See their productivity increase accordingly.
5. Notice significantly improved public perceptions of the
    federal government as a whole.

The government invests no special effort to turn ordinary federal employees into brand ambassadors. And they don't have to. The integrity of individual federal employees already acts as a kind of "reputation insurance" for the apparatus of government as a whole. The only thing that needs to happen is removal of artificial barriers to communication with the public.

97

Permanent Disbelief & Its Impact On Government Public Affairs

"Permanent Spin" has an eye-catching headline but the Weekly Standard article makes a pretty routine claim: You can't trust the government.

This article in particular focused on political PR, criticizing the Administration for refusing to label several terrorist attacks for what they were. Jibes like this fly from both sides of the aisle and in popular culture; even *Saturday Night Live* joined the fray with a satirical skit mocking a candidate for secretly taped remarks at a fundraiser that undermined his carefully crafted public messaging.

Sometimes political PR goes off-the-cuff, and people can't decide whether it's a good thing or bad. The *New York Times* reported on the angst within the party that followed unscripted remarks at a national political convention. *The New Republic* had mixed reviews but admitted that it could be "accidental political genius." Others said flat out that it was in fact "genius," no miscalculation at all.

In the civil service there is PR too, but we call it "public affairs." People don't trust that either. A good example is the explosion of conspiracy theories surrounding a posting by the Social Security Administration of their intent to buy 174,000 hollow-point bullets. (Not just bullets mind you but "hollow-point," which sound extra-scary for an Agency you think of as primarily in the business of distributing elderly people the savings they worked for all those years.)

According to FBO.gov the solicitation was posted on August 7, 2012. A keyword search on Google of "social security" and "bullets" for the dates August 7-15 yielded more than 7,000 results. The article at Business Insider had a typical introductory paragraph with alarm bells:

> *"First the DHS needed 450 million rounds of ammunition, then the NOAA requested 46,000 rounds, now we've discovered an online request at FBO.gov calling for 174,000 rounds of ammunition for the Social Security Administration (SSA)."*

Finally, a week after the original solicitation was posted, Social Security put an item in its blog (not on its homepage, nor Press Releases and News – explaining the the ammunition was for law enforcement and public safety purposes. (Note that there is no link that I can find from the Agency's website homepage to the blog.)

To put it mildly, the blog post did not exactly put out the flames of the conspiracy theory rumor mill, especially given the purchases of ammunition by other Federal agencies. Reported the Chicago Tribune:

> *Even late night talk show host Jay Leno joked, "What*

senior citizens are they worried about? I mean, who's going to storm the building?"

It was not untypical for the official response to be later rather than sooner. And it's not surprising that such a delayed reaction is ineffective.

What is hard to understand is this: If we know that people don't trust PR ("spinmeisters") in general, and they don't trust any representatives of government either, why do we continue to act as if the public hangs on our every word?

I would go so far as to say that the public is in a state of "permanent disbelief" at all official statements. Or perhaps "suspension of belief." Or "constant skepticism."

Call it what you want, it seems that it is time to match strategy with reality. If you know that you are abou to do something controversial or discordant with your audience's expectations of you (e.g., buy ammunition for an Agency that doesn't seem to be about law enforcement) then it makes sense to let people know ahead of time that you're about to do so.

But even that is not enough. If you know that your actions will be perceived skeptically, rather than defensively hide the explanation on a blog unlinked to your website, it makes sense to put a big and clear feature story on the homepage for a good week or two.

And when you put that feature story out there, it's probably also a good idea to add some facts, figures, historical examples, and other concrete data out that show you have a really good reason for doing what you did.

Plus make a senior official available for interviews to respond. Anything from mainstream media, to bloggers, to daytime talkshows and late night TV – wherever the audience goes. Yes, even to outlets that are critical of you – especially those!

While it's impossible to completely defuse skepticism about the validity of government communication, it is absolutely possible, necessary and required to do a better job of talking with our audience rather than at them. The goal is never to make up stories or mislead, but rather to promote a positive working relationship unfettered by secret doubts about what's going on behind the scenes.

Good PR is ethical PR, and that includes being transparent as much as security concerns will allow. There's nothing wrong with engaging an Agency's critics. In fact, that is the very definition of citizen engagement – to go where the issues are, not just for the feel-good outreach campaign hurrahs.

98

Why Agencies Need A "Chief Conversationalist"

Recently I read that people trust federal employees, but they don't trust the federal government as a whole. According to survey after survey, trust in this institution is at an "all time low."

From a common sense point of view, it's not really hard to know why. The public regularly depends on our huge infrastructure to function. But of course it doesn't always do that, or people disagree about...well just about everything.

But then agencies make a neutral-to-bad situation worse – by being notoriously closemouthed about responding to criticism.

(There are some exceptions, like the Transportation Safety Administration, probably because they have an unpleasant but necessary job involving so many customers every single day. This story about their partnership with a hotel chain to reduce tension at checkpoints is a must-read.)

It's not that they don't know what people are saying. They do, at least to some extent. But that fact alone does not solve everything:

- Budget cuts have led to homemade news clips, which are dominated by traditional media, selectively chosen and don't tell you whether most coverage is positive or negative, or why.
- Social media news clips are unsophisticated or there is a perception that social media is "not real" or populated by extremists, e.g. "crazy people."
- Providing negative feedback can get you in trouble – I have actually had someone caution me, "Be careful that people don't think you are disloyal for sharing this stuff." (And I've also seen myself quoted on a public message board with the insinuation that I'm a government propagandist.)
- Some tend to shrug off valid criticism as "just more or the same" or "ignorance."

All of this is really just denial that listening is important, and that what our stakeholders think of us matters, and that we cannot control it. The denial comes from defensiveness – fear.

Agencies tend to equate listening to criticism, acknowledging it, and talking about it as equivalent to admitting they have done something wrong. It seems like a strange phenomenon, especially when you consider that government leaders and ordinary employees are extraordinarily dedicated to and passionate about helping the public.

But unfortunately, the fear is based in reality, as feds are regularly bashed in public and confronted by a lot of red tape as well. Former Harvard University president Larry Summers has commented about the daunting nature of public service as a career (of course, this as a political's perspective):

> "The fact that it takes so long to be confirmed by the Senate, the fact that you have to go through the financial equivalent of a colonoscopy to enter government . . . The fact that there are so many rules and restrictions and bits of hostility towards those who are in government."

Conversely, the public does not understand the nature of federal government communication.

- For one thing, Agency officials and their representatives are very careful about what they say. They cannot talk "off the cuff." Words have weight, the weight of history and official record. And there are many consultations about the way that speech is made.
- There is also coordination across agencies, and between civil servants and political appointees, to coordinate and keep Agency speech consistent.

All of this is why Open Government is so critically important to digital engagement, and communication.

- Simply releasing high-value data in a usable format bolsters trust and credibility in and of itself.
- On this front, my experience has been that (contrary to popular stereotypes) the "politicals" want agencies to move forward, get the data out there, share as much as possible, now.

- It's not just words, but absolute credo among every person I've seen speak, or spoken with directly.

I'm not saying bad things never happen – scandals. Of course they do. But the reality I see is much more banal.

You know what people say to me, when they hear what I do?

- "Tell your agency to make records management a more logical process."
- "Tell me how I can find these images you have in the catalog, that only have a description of a location, but no actual JPEG attached."
- "I visited NARA one time, I was looking for information on my grandfather."

There it is...and what happened? Some is good, some is bad, and nobody is going to die. Engagement, feedback, interaction, and dialogue have to be a normal thing. Criticism doesn't bite. We have to get used to hearing it and dealing with it in a way that's productive.

Within the Agency, there is also a key distinction to be made between related activities, and a critical realization to be made.

- Digital engagement is not communication in and of itself. It is the act of facilitating communication across online channels, broadening access to all interested parties.
- You can judge the quality of digital engagement by the number of conversations, the substantive quality of those conversations, and how well they filter into the agency and back out to the public.

- Failure to listen, engage and "conversate" creates a self-fulfilling prophecy. Silence or awkward, stuttering responses create assumptions – incompetence or a great big conspiracy to control the world.

Any fear-based strategy doesn't work.

With respect to engagement and communication, it only leads to this kind of thinking as a trigger-fire response: "Don't add fuel to the fire."

The downstream consequence is "outreach" and "digital engagement" that shies away from substantive issues and toward non-controversial education. Sophisticated technology – flashy social media tools, the latest and greatest mobile apps, multimedia presentations – become a substitute for the real conversation the public wants. A waste of time if it doesn't move the needle.

So actually, the best thing a government engagement specialist can do is to be a channel for what people are saying – both on the outside and on the inside.

This "chief conversationalist" (digital engagement lead or director) listens, connects, validates that the sentiments are real – thus bringing inflamed emotions down, and facilitating a rational dialogue. This person does not have to be a subject matter expert – in fact it is better if they are not – because the goal is to hear what other people are saying without personal bias as to whether it is relevant.

Great engagement yields improvement in the way agencies work, better-served citizens, and more efficient and effective government as a whole.

XXII

Work/Life Balance

99

Slow Down: You're Probably Screwing Up

I did this crazy thing the other day. It was so out of character. I went to the library.

They had a shelf called "great reads." I went over to it and ran my hand along the modest beat-up walnut. One book stood out. It was old, but I'd always wanted to read it.

New notifications said my cellphone, and then it started beeping. *Texts.* Annoyed, I put it away.

As a kid, time seemed to crawl. Now, many years later, I realize the value of slowing down.

This month's Harvard Business Review has a cover story called "Managing the High-Intensity Workplace." It's about the strategies people use to deal with an unreasonably demanding environment, which is to say most workplaces these days.

Briefly, most people:

- Go along and lose their personal lives;
- Pretend to go along and burn out along the way, ulti-

mately burning out from the stress; or
- Admit that they're not automatons and get punished.

Boy, have things changed in just a few decades. And there isn't even a reward for it.

Why exactly are we in school day and night, chasing degrees that yield debt but not a job?

Why are we ignoring our families to work on...you name it. Why don't we make marriages and kids our first priority? (No time.) Why are so many people divorced and then in unhappy relationships?

Why are so many people loudly unhappy at work, toxic to themselves and their colleagues?

Why are so many people quietly unhappy, constantly answering this email and that email, doing this project and that? Without any thanks or appreciation. No reward other than "you get to keep your job?"

It's a sunny day today and I enjoyed feeling the sun on my face, the wind blowing soft and fresh across my body.

If we could just slow down a little bit and leave ourselves alone. We'd be happier and more productive, too.

Here, I give you permission.

100

Only Superheroes Need Apply

I was talking with a friend over the weekend about her anniversary plans. "You doing anything nice?"

Really I was just making conversation. What with jobs, kids and errands, not to mention watching the money, most couples don't do the splurge.

"No, not really," she said, as expected.

My friend has younger kids and we're heading into the empty-nester phase. I remembered how very badly I had wanted help as a young mother. It was hard to be responsible all the time. I longed to go out with my husband to the movies, just the two of us. But there was nobody we trusted to watch the kids, and even if we had, the cost of dinner and a movie and a babysitter was a barrier.

"Let me take the kids for a few hours," I impulsively offered, as I had no idea what I would do with her kids. "I'm not doing anything tomorrow."

Just then, one of her kids ran up to her. "Mommy, Mommy, look at this!"

He had a storybook in his hands with "Minions" characters

all over it. Then he started talking, blah, blah, blah.

It wasn't very interesting to me, but I could see she was trying to follow. "That's great, honey! Yeah…"

To me it looked like she was drowning, drowning in a pool.

She turned toward me. I could see her assembling her smile like a mask.

"That's okay, but thank you. It's sweet of you to offer."

Running, her son was running all around the room and she darted off.

I wonder when it was that we became so goddamn perfect. When did we decide to set that bar for performance so high, so impossibly high? We have to be the impossibly perfect parents, the impossibly perfect lovers, the impossibly perfect ones at work.

Why?

Lots of resumes have come across my desk over the years. In roughly the past five, there's been a noticeable shift away from listing responsibilities and accomplishments. Instead, many communicators have a column on the right that simply shows all the skills and software packages they've mastered.

And there is more. They also have personal websites, and portfolios online. They have freelance jobs, their own companies. They have bachelor's degrees, and master's degrees, and certifications.

They're overqualified, they have pushed and pushed and made themselves into the Barbie dolls of communications excellence, even though the #1 qualification of all is someone I can trust, who can stop and critically *think*.

Relationships, too, have become so unforgiving.

My grandparents, on both sides (may they rest in peace), stuck together for many decades, through war and trauma and poverty. They didn't always get along. But they didn't make such a big *deal* about everything.

If they competed at times, it was usually over who the grandchildren loved more. My father's parents would ask if I preferred my mother's parents and vice-versa.

I remember that Grandma, my mother's mother, always tried to reduce the pressure on me. When we visited them, and I left the Sabbath table after an hour and laid down to rest on the couch, my father would follow me and get me up.

"Come back to the table," he used to say. "Your *seat* is waiting."

And before I could say "please stop anthropomorphizing," Grandma would appear.

"Alex," she wagged a finger in his face. "G-d is everywhere. Would you please not make such an ISSUE!"

I have to laugh. I loved her so much. Grandma, wherever you are, I love you.

The modern religious Jewish community has far, far exceeded any kind of discipline my father tried to impose. The rules have exploded, they are enormous, it is impossible for me to keep any sort of track.

And then there is dating. Which I observe from a distance, watching my kids and their peers growing up and trying to mate. I don't remember anything like this kind of pressure in my life – to be thin, and beautifully made up, and an academic super-achiever, with an internship, who has independently invented a mobile app with which to save the world.

And all of this pressure hitting before you even hit puberty!

No wonder our children are becoming anxious, depressed, and increasingly resistant to the over-prescribed path we call "progression" up the educational ladder.

> About one-third of U.S. college students had dif-
> ficulty functioning in the last 12 months due to
> depression, and almost half said they felt over-
> whelming anxiety in the last year, according to the
> 2013 National College Health Assessment, which
> examined data from 125,000 students from more
> than 150 colleges and universities. – 2013 National
> College Health Assessment via the American Psy-
> chological Association

I have to wonder, is the increasing willingness to medicate school-age children solely reflective of better medical care? Or is it little more than a socially sanctioned method of blocking their normal responses to abnormal social expectations?

Meaning, what if we simply cut the number of hours they have to sit in a chair, ended standardized testing and replaced it with narrative annual evaluations, eliminated homework and simply let them go out to the backyard and play?

Business leaders are under a similarly mounting pressure. In the past – and believe me this was not a perfect system, but it was clear and reliable – it was enough to run a business and make a profit. Over time, the expectations grew to include a certain amount of corporate social responsibility, and then grew again to cover employee engagement. These expectations make sense and to a certain extent are, of course, reasonable – from a return-on-investment perspective, and frankly also ethically.

But it is not reasonable to expect any human being to assume the qualities of an omnipotent being. And this, I think, is where business has gone off the rails.

It is not possible for any human being to be endlessly

inspiring, perfectly humane, super-fantastically creative, innovating constantly, disruptively, and in a revolutionary manner, infinitely, all the time, in a never-ending explosion of perfect leadership skills.

It is not possible.

In the world of branding we speak of this term "positioning," meaning that the brand occupies a very distinct, very relevant, very compelling and consistent place in the customer's mind.

A very distinct and singular place.

Not all places, for to do so would be not only impossible but would eliminate from the customer's mind that space within which the brand itself, in all its equity, has lodged itself like a rock, hopefully.

No – you want the brand to be simple, to be limited, to be singular and to be good at whatever that particular brand can do.

The same principle applies to ourselves, to our roles as parents, to our work, to our relationships, to our religious practice, to whatever extent we want to have one, and to the leaders who shape our world.

We've got to stop expecting ourselves, and everyone we deal with, to live up to some kind of superpower mold. It doesn't exist. It is impossible. It's unrealistic and it hurts us as long as we can't let it go.

We've got to let it go.

If we could allow ourselves to be human, if we could stop punishing people for the inescapable fact that human beings are born to learn through making mistakes, that would really, really be a good thing.

If we could stop expecting perfection of ourselves, maybe

we would be a little less defensive about the mistakes we invariably do make.

Opening up a space for really good dialogue about what kind of people we are, who we want to be.

Making it okay to put your feet up on the couch and do nothing for a few hours while a friend takes the kids and similarly, does nothing very special in particular.

Bringing the joy of living back to this increasingly frantic setting on an imaginary treadmill, that we have come to experience as "life" in the default.

About the Author

Dr. Dannielle Blumenthal is a wife, mother and Patriot. A lifelong writer, she has authored many books on topics such as feminist theory, popular culture, branding and marketing, cultural polarization, propaganda, empowerment, and personal memoir. The views expressed are her own and do not represent a federal agency or the government as a whole.

As a branding specialist, Dr. Blumenthal is known for her focus on the humanization of impervious entities. In straight-forward terms, brands need to connect with customers on a personal level in order to build deeper, more meaningful relationships that promote their affinity and loyalty. She has written extensively on this topic, advocating for strategies that prioritize transparency, vulnerability, and emotional intelligence.

As an advocate, she strongly believes that "the personal is political." In addition, for a citizen to engage in action-oriented research, resilience is essential. To that end, Dr. Blumenthal encourages people to engage in a journey of personal growth and development through reflection, self-care, and mindfulness.

Most important of all, Dr. Blumenthal believes in surrendering to God, and accordingly, that one's work should bring honor to Him and serve the mission He has given us in life.

Dr. Blumenthal holds a Ph.D. in sociology from the Graduate School and University Center of the City University of New York and a graduate certificate in organizational development from Fielding Graduate University.

You can connect with me on:

🌐 https://www.dannielleblumenthal.com

www.ingramcontent.com/pod-product-compliance
Lightning Source LLC
Chambersburg PA
CBHW070940250726
48663CB00001B/1